Sunrise reflections in water-filled potholes, Green River overlook, Canyonlands National Park, Utah.

Rhododendron and redwoods, Lady Bird Johnson Grove, Redwood National Park, California.

WILD BY LAW

Tidal flat, Seymour Canal, Admiralty Island National Monument, Alaska.

WILD BY LAW

THE SIERRA CLUB LEGAL DEFENSE FUND
AND THE PLACES IT HAS SAVED

Photographs by C A R R C L I F T O N
and other contributors

Text by T O M T U R N E R

Sierra Club Legal Defense Fund
in association with Sierra Club Books
San Francisco

Library of Congress Cataloging in Publication Data
Turner, Tom.
    Wild by law: the Sierra Club Legal Defense Fund and the
places it has saved / by Tom Turner: with photographs by
Carr Clifton.
    ISBN 0-87156-627-3
    1. Sierra Club. Legal Defense Fund.   2. Wilderness areas—
Law and legislation—United States.   3. Envronmental law—
United States.
KF5635.T87   1990
346.7304'6782—dc20
[347.30646782]   89-78349
                                     CIP

Cover photo: *The Watchman and the Virgin River,
    Zion National Park, Utah.*

Editorial and production supervision by *Diana Landau
    Publishing Services*
Jacket and book design by *Herman + Company, San Francisco*
Maps by *EarthSurface Graphics*
Typography by *Mark Woodworth, San Francisco*
Printed by *Dai Nippon Printing Company, Ltd., Tokyo*

10 9 8 7 6 5 4 3 2 1

Contents

Kaweah Peaks, Sequoia National Park, California.

Acknowledgments

Many people gave generously of their time and recollections for this project, and I am grateful to them all. In addition to the people below, I made extensive use of the work of John Harper (*Mineral King: Public Concern With Government Policy,* Pacifica Press, 1982), M. Rupert Cutler (doctoral dissertation on the litigation over Mineral King and three other Forest Service matters, University of Michigan, 1972), Susan Schrepfer (*The Fight to Save the Redwoods,* University of Wisconsin Press, 1983), and the splendid annual series of *Wildlife Reports* published by the National Audubon Society.

Those who consented to interviews or helped in other ways include Lauri Adams, Phil Barnett, Reginald Barrett, Phil Berry, Joe Brecher, Dave Brower, Bill Curtiss, Bob Dreher, Fred Fisher, Howard Fox, Ed Gambell, Rich Gordon, Don Harris, John Hoffman, Hans Hollitscher, Doug Honnold, Bob Jasperson, Eric Jorgensen, K. J. Metcalf, Martin Litton, Cliff Lobaugh, Warren Matthews, Mike McCloskey, Jim Moorman, Lori Potter, Kim Ramos, Gordon Robinson, Tony Ruckel, John Sacklin, Lee Selna, Karin Sheldon, Vic Sher, Mike Sherwood, Andy Stahl, Todd True, Ed Wayburn, Ron Wilson, Corrie Yackulic, Durwood Zaelke, and Marjorie Ziegler. Thanks to them all.

Most of all I'm indebted to Rick Sutherland, who dreamed up the project, asked me to take it on, and helped immeasurably in the preparation of the manuscript; Buck Parker, daily sounding board, advisor, and running partner; Jon Beckmann and Danny Moses of Sierra Club Books, who believed at once in the idea and offered nothing but encouragement; and Diana Landau, who helped in the conception of the book, found the photographer, edited the manuscript, engaged the designer, hired the printer, and made the project happen. Without her, all we'd have is a fat manuscript and a pile of transparencies.

Finally, I dedicate my portion of the book to my wife, Mary Jorgensen, stalwart supporter throughout.

T. T.

Foreword

The catalyst role that environmental law has played in bringing ecological values into the forefront of American life is an untold story that offers fascinating insights into the decision-making process of our politics. Part of this fascination derives from the circumstance that twenty-five years ago there was no environmental law, there were no environmental lawyers, and ordinary citizens did not have a right to present their causes and complaints in our courts of law.

The Sierra Club Legal Defense Fund has played a major role in changing those circumstances. In his biography of this aggressive, trailblazing organization, Tom Turner describes the swift, stunning impact that environmental law has made on our institutions and on the nation's conservation policies. This vivid, informative book also makes us aware that the real "clients" of environmental lawyers are unborn generations: any story of a major environmental lawsuit is a true-life drama about a running fight to enhance the overall environment by preserving the air, the water, or some imperiled parcel of the American earth.

Turner's account of the Legal Defense Fund's thirteen-year fight to save Mineral King valley and preserve it unimpaired in Sequoia National Park (where it had always belonged) is a dramatic high point of this book. I was a participant in this swirling controversy, which, when launched by the Sierra Club in 1965, had all the earmarks of a hopeless cause. Their opponent was Walt Disney, then a secular American saint. In short order California's governor, Ronald Reagan, and officials in high places in our nation's capital were uttering hosannahs in support of Disney's plan to turn this secluded valley into the world's largest, most elaborate ski resort.

This book is valuable for lawyers and lay readers alike as an introduction to the vicissitudes and opportunities of environmental litigation. We learn, for example, how "defeats" in the courts sometimes end as tactical victories. The Mineral King saga also informs us about the process through which one of the landmark principles of environmental law — the right of ordinary citizens to present their causes in the courts of law — evolved out of the United States Supreme Court's deliberations over legal issues raised by Legal Defense Fund lawyers in the Disney case.

Chapter by chapter, this volume traces the emergence of environmental law as a major force in the life of our nation. It demonstrates how, in a few short years, resourceful lawyers have used the law as a device to further ecological reforms and help put environmental values on the cutting edge of social change. It shows, too, how the National Environmental Policy Act of 1970 was transformed by lawyers and judges into the most important resource-planning law ever enacted by the Congress. Decisions by federal courts concerning the act gave conservationists a powerful tool they could use to force federal officials to evaluate the ecological impacts of significant new activities. Other action-examples cited by the author reveal how the Legal Defense Fund and other environmental law firms were able to break new ground in challenging the stewardship of big bureaucracies over complex issues and to force lethargic officials to take action to protect the land and the public health.

These changes have wrought a triumph of participatory democracy that has broad ramifications for the future. Unlike European nations, where — in both communist and noncommunist countries — designated bureaucrats make most vital decisions about the environment, in the United States today environmental law guides and constrains the conduct of most public officials. It impacts policymaking at all levels of government, and its doctrines have put ecologists in a position where they can now monitor and guide the enforcement and implementation of the nation's growing body of laws governing the conservation of resources.

For two decades, environmental attorneys have been shock troops in skirmishes that have altered public policymaking and changed the way citizens use their power to influence decisions about resources in this country. Environmental law is still evolving: indeed, it is now likely that this discipline will be in the vanguard as the nation responds to the national and worldwide environmental challenges of the twenty-first century.

Stewart L. Udall
Former Secretary of the Interior
Santa Fe, New Mexico

Sawgrass and cypress, Big Cypress National Preserve, Florida.

President's Preface

In the late 1960s public interest law firms arrived on the American legal scene. One of the first of these was the Sierra Club Legal Defense Fund, launched in 1971 to represent conservationists in environmental litigation. *Wild by Law* describes a number of important cases brought by the lawyers of the Sierra Club Legal Defense Fund during the past two decades.

I have had the privilege of being involved in the practice of environmental law since its earliest days. I have observed firsthand the imaginative efforts of able litigators across the country as they created a body of law to protect America's natural resources and improve the quality of its environment. Throughout the 1970s and 1980s, lawyers have been at the forefront of the environmental movement. I agree with David Sive, an early pioneer in the field, who asserts that "in no other political and social movement has litigation played such an important and dominant role."

Environmental litigation has been both the last resort to preserve threatened natural resources and the cutting edge to establish new precedents and important legal principles. Lawsuits have saved millions of acres of public lands from inappropriate development, sometimes with injunctions that halted bulldozers and chainsaws virtually at the last minute.

I know from my own experience that without litigation many public lands now protected for future generations in national parks and wilderness areas would have been irreparably damaged. As described herein, Admiralty Island in southeast Alaska would now be well on its way to being a clearcut wasteland instead of a national monument; Mineral King valley in the southern Sierra would be a ski resort instead of part of Sequoia National Park; and the great national parks of southern Utah would be surrounded by industrial development and blanketed by polluted air.

Litigation has also protected hundreds of species of plants and animals threatened with extinction by preserving essential habitat and eliminating threats to their continued existence.

Successful lawsuits have helped to improve air and water quality. They have forced polluting companies to clean up their discharges and pay civil penalties for past violations. Some of these lawsuits have resulted in creative settlements, as polluters agreed to pay money into court-approved trust funds to mitigate the adverse impacts of the pollution or to acquire and protect important wetlands or wildlife habitat.

Litigation has also forced the government to do its job. Environmental lawyers representing concerned citizens have compelled the executive branch of government to do what the legislative branch has directed. Without such litigation, strong environmental pronouncements would be virtually meaningless.

There is no fundamental reason to believe that environmental litigation will be less important in the future. To the contrary, I am firmly convinced that much more of it will be necessary to meet the increasing environmental challenges we will face in the years ahead. Pollution and depletion of natural resources are occurring on a vast and historically unprecedented scale. The worldwide use of fossil fuels has increased ten times in the twentieth century, and the atmosphere now contains 25 percent more carbon dioxide than it did in 1900. Each year 200 million tons of sulfur dioxide and oxides of nitrogen are added to the atmosphere.

This and other pollution has caused serious threats to the earth's ozone layer and has led to the buildup of "greenhouse" gases in the atmosphere. Gus Speth, president of the World Resource Institute, states that "these closely linked assaults on the atmosphere probably constitute the most serious pollution threats in history."

And the future doesn't look promising. By the middle of the next century, the world's population is expected to increase from the current five billion to ten billion. By that time, the world economy is projected to be five to ten times as large as today's $13 trillion. It is going to be difficult in the extreme to achieve a cleaner, more healthy environment in the face of the threats to our natural resources implicit in these projected population increases and vast economic expansion.

I share Gus Speth's belief that the driving force for a cleaner, more livable world will come "from the hopes and fears of people, from their wonder at the natural world, from their dogged insistence that some things that seem very wrong are just that. . . ." And I believe he is right when he says that "politicians around the world are increasingly hearing the demand that things be set right."

If they are, it is none too soon. Time is getting short. A well-known riddle poses the following problem: if a lily pond contains a single leaf on the first day and every day the number of leaves doubles, when is the pond half full if it is completely full in thirty days? The answer is the twenty-ninth day. There is increasing concern among many thoughtful people that humanity is in the twenty-ninth day of its stay on Earth and that we have very little, if any, time left to set things right.

I believe that the courts will continue to have an important role in helping to set things right, particularly here in America, where we now have a twenty-year tradition of rigorous interpretation of the laws passed by Congress and the state legislatures. For its part, the Sierra Club Legal Defense Fund plans to expand its efforts to ensure that this tradition will continue. To this end, the organization has opened a new office in Florida and hopes to open one in the Midwest in the near future. Legal Defense Fund lawyers are also beginning to bring lawsuits to address environmental problems that go beyond national boundaries, that are international in scope.

In these new ventures the Sierra Club Legal Defense Fund

is guided by the spirit of Justice William O. Douglas, the best environmentalist who has ever served on the United States Supreme Court. That spirit was nowhere better articulated than in his dissenting opinion in the Mineral King case, described at length in the first chapter of *Wild by Law*. The old judge argued for an expanded concept of the legal doctrine of "standing to sue" in order to protect natural resources.

> The voice of the inanimate object . . . should not be stilled . . . before these priceless bits of Americana (such as a valley, an alpine meadow, a river, or a lake) are forever lost or are so transformed as to be reduced to the eventual rubble of our urban environment, the voice of the existing beneficiaries of these environmental wonders should be heard.

> Perhaps they will not win. Perhaps the bulldozers of "progress" will plow under all the aesthetic wonders of this beautiful land. That is not the present question. The sole question is, who has standing to be heard?

> Those who hike the Appalachian Trail into Sunfish Pond, New Jersey, and camp or sleep there, or the Allagash in Maine, or climb the Guadalupes in West Texas, or who canoe and portage the Quetico Superior in Minnesota, certainly should have standing to defend these natural wonders before courts or agencies, though they live 3,000 miles away.

While the concept of standing articulated by Justice Douglas has not been embraced by the courts in America, his ideas live on. Lawyers of the Sierra Club Legal Defense Fund have brought successful cases to prevent the extinction of endangered wildlife. Two of these cases, *Palila* v. *Hawaii Department of Land and Natural Resources* and *Northern Spotted Owl* v. *Hodel* were brought in the names of the species at risk. Justice Douglas would be proud.

The fact is that the American public is vastly more attuned to environmental values then ever before. Such problems as global warming, ozone depletion, acid rain, water pollution, energy conservation, the destruction of old-growth forests, and the extinction of species are no longer regarded as fringe concerns. Environmental quality and the protection of natural resources are coming to be seen for what they are: critical for the maintenance of life on this planet. To those resources and to the lawyers who fight for them, this book is dedicated.

Fredric P. Sutherland
President
Sierra Club Legal Defense Fund

Photographer's Note

When I was eleven years old I hiked out of Mineral King with a pack of brothers, cousins, parents, and friends. The adults of our troop had the good sense and inspiration to take their two families of boys out of the valley oak country where we lived and into the high, rugged terrain above and surrounding Mineral King. We still refer to that trip as "our wild time," and such it was. We were a restless and curious bunch, and we needed wildness. Besides, our friends were members of the Sierra Club. They said that the Disney Corporation had plans to develop a giant ski resort and Disney village there at Mineral King, and that the Sierra Club was trying to protect the valley and the adjacent backcountry of Sequoia National Park. The Club needed our help—everyone's help—and the best way to help was first to get to know Mineral King.

I remember our literally breathtaking hike over Timber Gap and the more gradual ascent to Pinto Lake, where we set up our rough but idyllic family camp. There were fish, bear, and the calling of coyotes at night. I remember the chill of the thin alpine air, the evening glow on granite cliffs, and the liquid sound of water so cold, clear, and pure that we drank from every lake and stream. As long as we didn't harm anything—birds, marmots, pikas, flowers, or trees—and as long as we didn't wash our dishes or ourselves directly in the stream, we were free to be as wild as we pleased. To me this was paradise. It was one of the happiest times of my young life.

Though I'd lived most of my years in the country, the freedom I experienced that summer above Mineral King, the dawning consciousness that I was a member of a biological community, and the awareness that my behavior would affect it, were all new to me. That summer I was initiated into a deeper and richer relationship with the natural world, a relationship that developed my sensibility as a photographer.

The sentimental talking animals and make-believe landscapes of Disney fantasies suddenly seemed threatening, both to me and to the vital new world I had discovered at timberline. It was *real* life, *real* sound and landscapes that moved me. No one had to tell me that a Disney village in these or any mountains would be a nightmare for the real, living beings there. At the age of eleven I couldn't articulate this growing awareness of my membership in and love for the natural world.

I only knew I had made important discoveries: that I preferred wilderness to any make-believe, and that a living landscape was more full of wonder than fiction could ever be.

Everyone in my family joined the Sierra Club when we returned home that summer, and I was proud to sleep next to my new Sierra Club membership card that I'd pinned to the wall next to my bed. It was 1968, the year before the Sierra Club filed the first lawsuit to stop the desecration of Mineral King.

My youthful explorations of the Sierra Nevada high country and my intoxication with its glowing light and living mountains led me in the direction of landscape photography. Now, with my camera, I continue to explore this nation's remaining wild country. I know more clearly than I ever imagined in my youth how few and precious are these last wild places, and how vulnerable they are. Some of the places I've photographed in the last decade have been so degraded by logging, dams, or development that I can't bear to return to them. But Mineral King is one of the places I come back to again and again. More than twenty years have passed since my first trip to that great U-shaped valley with its crown of peaks, and it is still the magical place I remember from the family visit long ago. For that I am thankful and always will be.

If the adults in my younger life had lacked the desire to introduce me to wilderness, I might never have known it as home. I am grateful to all the people who teach children to appreciate wilderness and wildlife. I am indebted to the lawyers and staff of the Sierra Club Legal Defense Fund, whose vision, diligence, unswerving commitment, and persevering hope help to protect the last wild, living places, and to the thousands of men, women, and young people who donate their time, resources, and inspiration to help protect and restore our natural environment.

I would like to give special thanks to Deanne Henninger for her support, assistance, and patience throughout this project. I would also like to thank Steve Swadley for assisting with the muscle work on Admiralty Island and for the many salmon feasts we enjoyed there.

Carr Clifton
Taylorsville, California

Maple and birch in fall colors along an unnamed brook, Adirondack Park and Preserve, New York.

Introduction

This book is a celebration of some of the places on the American earth that have been left more or less in their original condition, to be passed intact to future generations, through the work of the men and women of the Sierra Club Legal Defense Fund. It is a selective history; it makes no pretense of being comprehensive. The battles described herein—for Mineral King, for Admiralty Island, for the Colorado Plateau, and the rest—were also waged by dozens of organizations and thousands of individuals. This book highlights the part that litigation played in those fights.

Readers may note that many of these legal campaigns ended in what the rigorous observer must count as defeats, at least within the courtroom. Yet the ultimate result was in all cases victory, sometimes total, sometimes something less. We leave it to readers to draw their conclusions, but would suggest that compiling a simple scorecard of wins and losses in the various skirmishes that make up a major campaign of litigation may be misleading. What happens on the ground is what matters.

Litigation is perhaps the most powerful tool in the conservation cause. It allows ordinary citizens to confront far more powerful adversaries in industry and government and forces them to play by common rules. And it can prolong battles until the public at large becomes aware of the dispute and can work its will through its elected representatives.

At Mineral King, for example, the plaintiffs lost their procedural point before the United States Supreme Court, but in the process established one of the most important principles of environmental law: that citizens have a right to take environmental disputes into the federal courts. The legal battle also alerted the public and the press to the issues involved at Mineral King and delayed the project sufficiently for public opinion to swing against the Disney project, and eventually to preserve the valley within Sequoia National Park.

Likewise, at Admiralty Island in southeast Alaska, the original lawsuit failed at the district court but was reinstated upon release of a biological study that supported many of the concerns voiced by the plaintiffs in the case. Again, the timetable for logging was lengthened and the timber company dropped its plans to clearcut much of the island. In the meantime, the public became sufficiently aroused to force the setting aside of most of the island as a wilderness national monument.

The Redwood National Park litigation led a federal judge to tell Congress that if it meant what it said in the law that created the park—namely, that the Interior Department should take steps to protect the park from outside logging—then Congress would have to finish the job itself: it was beyond the power of the courts to make Congress keep its own promises. The lawsuit was dismissed, but it generated enough heat and light to cause Congress to double the size of the park.

The lesson in all this is that litigation is usually a means, rarely an end in itself. It is a tool in the never-ending fight to preserve and restore the planet Earth. When wielded by skilled practitioners, litigation can succeed where other tools fail. It is the one means by which citizens can demand that their rights be respected, that their laws be enforced and obeyed. A congressman can ignore letters from his constituents; the Department of the Interior cannot ignore a complaint filed against it in a federal court. That's the unique strength of the American legal system: it puts power into the hands of the otherwise powerless. It is the final check against this country's becoming an oligarchy, a dictatorship, or worse. It is by no means perfect, but it's far and away the best such system in the world.

Legal protection of the environment is a recent development, one that has emerged and been rapidly refined in the last third of the twentieth century. It is the creation of Congress and the state legislatures acting in response to an increasingly concerned citizenry. It is also the creation of the courts acting in response to arguments advanced by brilliant and committed lawyers, many of them barely out of law school.

Their timing was just right. As you look through this book, bear in mind that the places you see would not look the way they do but for timely intervention by inventive attorneys working for the Sierra Club Legal Defense Fund or its progenitors. In some places there would have been massive development. In others the trees and wildlife would have been decimated. In still others the skies would have been fouled with noxious pollutants.

As we said earlier, lawyers and lawsuits did not save these places by themselves. But had they not played their part in the battles, the places surely would have been lost.

A prominent friend, when told about the plan to create this book, said "I have only one piece of advice—call it volume one." We declined the suggestion, being slightly superstitious from having seen many "volumes one" or "first installments" be also the last. We hope, however, that we will come to regret the decision. There are two reasons for this, one of pride and the other of reality. First, we hope the Sierra Club Legal Defense Fund will continue to rack up significant legal victories and thus add to the gallery of photogenic places the organization has been instrumental in protecting. Second, alas, there is absolutely no indication at the end of the twentieth century that the drive to raze the forests, pave the meadows, foul the rivers, and sully the atmosphere will slacken any time soon. The need for the Sierra Club Legal Defense Fund is certain to continue. The organization will be there to meet the need.

Tom Turner
Berkeley, California

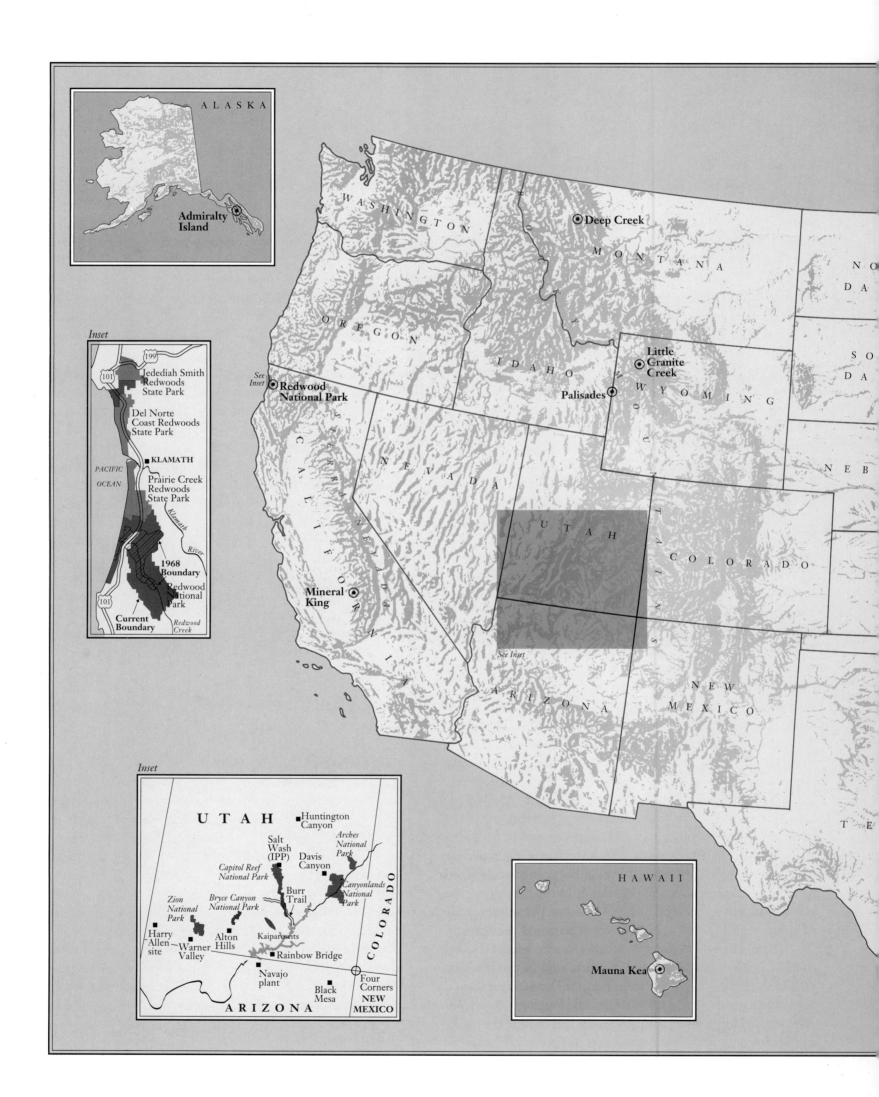

Cases Described in this Book

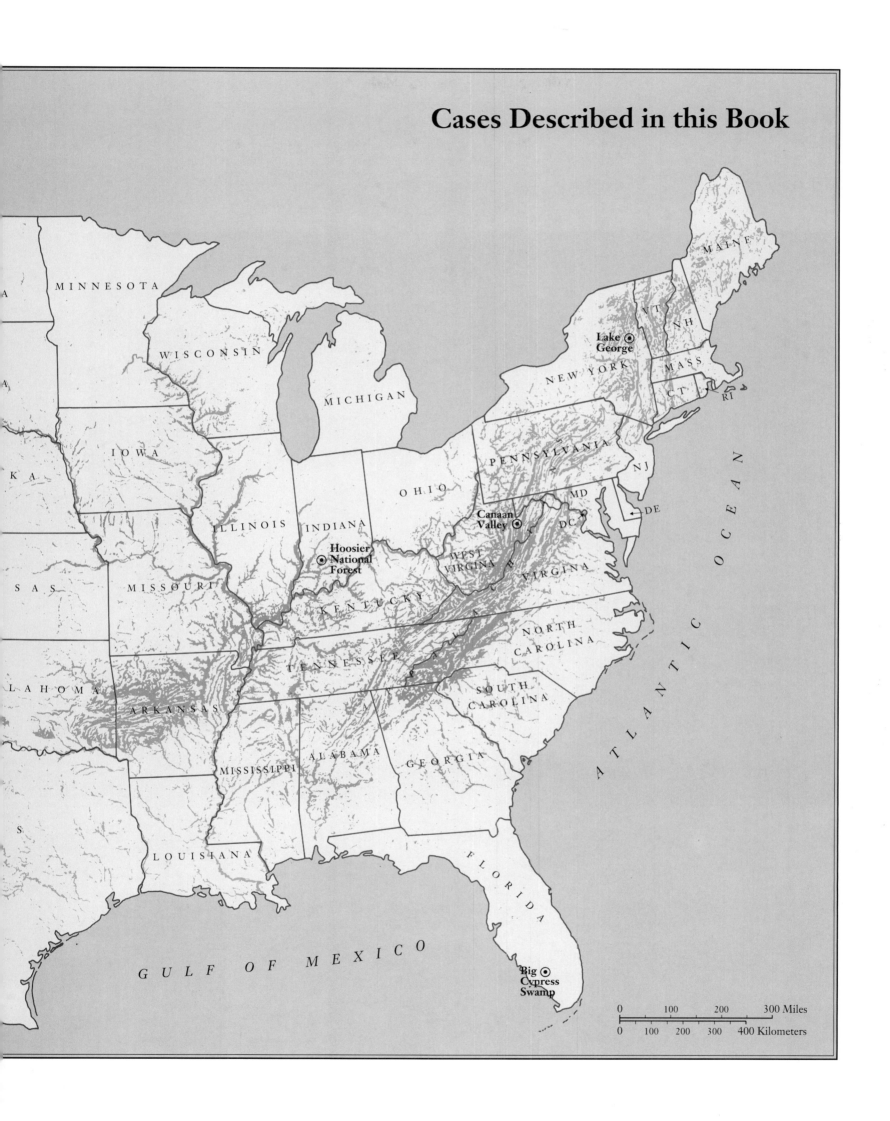

MINNESOTA

WISCONSIN

MICHIGAN

IOWA

MAINE

VT

NH

MASS

CT

RI

NEW YORK

Lake
George ⊙

PENNSYLVANIA

NJ

ILLINOIS

INDIANA

OHIO

MD

DE

MISSOURI

Hoosier
National
Forest ⊙

Canaan
Valley ⊙

WEST
VIRGINA

DC

VIRGINA

SAS

KENTUCKY

NORTH
CAROLINA

ATLANTIC OCEAN

LAHOMA

ARKANSAS

TENNESSEE

SOUTH
CAROLINA

S.

MISSISSIPPI

ALABAMA

GEORGIA

LOUISIANA

FLORIDA

GULF OF MEXICO

Big ⊙
Cypress
Swamp

0	100	200	300 Miles
0	100	200	300	400 Kilometers

Ansel's Wall, at Precipice Lake, Sequoia National Park, California.

WILD BY LAW

CHAPTER ONE

Mineral King
And the Creation of the Sierra Club Legal Defense Fund

I n 1956, the Sierra Club made Walt Disney an honorary life member in gratitude for his films on wildlife, which enthralled a generation of Americans. A dozen years later, the Sierra Club launched its first major environmental lawsuit, to block the filmmaker's bid to build a gigantic ski resort in a remote valley in the Sierra Nevada of California. The ensuing contest would lead to one of the most important Supreme Court decisions ever rendered on environmental matters. It would also launch environmental organizations in a whole new direction—toward the courthouses of the United States.

At the southern end of the Sierra, just before a flank of the range swings west to join the Tehachapis, a tall, rugged ridge juts southwest—the Great Western Divide. To its east is the canyon of the Kern River, to the west lie the headwaters of the East Fork of the Kaweah. The valley drained by the creeks that join to form the East Fork is known as Mineral King.

Mineral King comes by its name through a bit of wishful thinking. In the

Old cabin in Mineral King valley, with Farewell Canyon in the distance, now in Sequoia National Park, California.

Abandoned mine shaft on Monarch Creek, Mineral King valley.

1860s, sheepherders, hunters, explorers, and other Europeans visited the valley, and many found outcrops of promising ores. In 1873 a Tulare County farmer named James A. Crabtree entered the valley from the south, guided, he said, by Indian apparitions. He discovered a deposit of silver ore in what came to be known as White Chief cirque and rushed to town to file a claim. He recruited four men to return to the valley; they filed more claims and formulated bylaws for what they dubbed the "Mineral King Mining District." Silver fever swept through Porterville, the county seat, and then rolled north through the valley, attracting prospectors from Visalia, Farmersville, Lemoore, Kaweah, Fresno, and eventually San Francisco. At the peak of mining activity at Mineral King, in 1879, there were as many as 300 miners working claims in the valley and the high bowls above it, another 100 people improving an old stock trail to handle the expected heavy traffic in ore wagons, and perhaps 200 more milling lumber, building cabins, and providing other services for the miners.

Despite the high hopes for the Mineral King silver deposits, however, the entire enterprise went bust by 1882. Cold and snowy winters made the mining season short and access treacherous. Avalanches made the work hazardous. The silver ore was said to be "rebellious," with an unusually high lead content, which required roasting before milling, a prohibitively expensive process. The valley was abandoned by the miners and nature was left to reclaim its own, to begin in its deliberate fashion to dismantle the cabins, fill in the shafts, and oxidize the trams and culverts and smelters and mills. Soon flowers and grasses and trees began to appear on bare, abandoned slopes. The valley still beckoned to campers, hikers, and fishermen, and a small resort community flourished into the twentieth century, but the heyday of the King was past.

Little is left now to evoke the short boom-town history of Mineral King, but what remained in 1890 was more than enough to keep the valley from being included in Sequoia National Park, created that year mainly to protect the groves of giant sequoias growing west and north of Mineral King at somewhat lower altitudes. Following the creation of the park and at the urging of John Muir and the year-old Sierra Club, President Benjamin Harrison in 1893 proclaimed a vast Sierra Forest Preserve that encompassed most of the western slope of the Sierra—6,400 square miles—in order to control the grazing, logging, and prospecting that were already playing havoc with the mountains. A dozen years later, the Forest Service was formed, and in 1908 the unwieldy Sierra Forest Preserve (by then renamed Sierra National Forest) was divided into three parts. Mineral King now resided in Sequoia National Forest.

Muir and the Sierra Club then mounted a major campaign to expand Sequoia National Park, so as to preserve the high granite wilderness of the central and southern Sierra. The struggle was a lengthy one with heavy resistance from miners, loggers, would-be dam builders, and the Forest Service. The original grand plan was whittled back several times. When the park eventually was enlarged in 1926—to approximately twice its original size—Mineral King was again left out. The valley was, however, transformed into the Sequoia National Game Refuge, to be managed in a manner that would protect wildlife and habitat.

Mineral King valley encompasses approximately 15,000 acres. It is a U-shaped valley typical of the Sierra, carved by glaciers and forested on its lower slopes. It harbors a diverse community of plants and animals, including such scarce species as bald eagles, peregrine falcons, pine martens, wolverines, and spotted owls. It is well within the range of the California condor, should that now-incarcerated bird ever again ply the skies of California.

The floor of Mineral King valley lies at about 7,800 feet above sea level. Sawtooth Peak, the highest peak on the ridge that surrounds the valley—the boundary between national park and game refuge—reaches 12,343 feet. Trails that lead from the valley floor into the high country in three directions range from fairly gentle to strenuous.

Since the 1860s, hunters, hikers, and fishermen visited Mineral King in the summer, just as Indians had done for hundreds of years before them. Visitation in winter, however, was rare, because of heavy snows that usually fill the valley from October through May. The road into Mineral King is still the old miners' wagon route, which snakes its way about twenty-five miles from the town of Hammond up the East Fork canyon and into the valley. Only the most ambitious of cross-country skiers visited the valley after October, joined in later years by infrequent tracked-vehicle riders and snowmobilers.

The hardy souls who did ski into Mineral King, however, reported a spectacular spot for skiing: high bowls that border the valley on three sides, deep powder snow, spectacular views. Skiing, following the Great Depression, was beginning to catch on in California.

After World War II, the Sierra Club decided to explore the Sierra in search of areas suitable for development as alpine skiing resorts. By that time the Donner Pass area was well served with resorts, as were Sonora Pass and Lake Tahoe. Only Mammoth Mountain, on the east side of the Sierra, provided expansive skiing opportunities for Southern Californians, and it took nearly eight hours to drive to Mammoth from Los Angeles. Accordingly, in 1947 David Brower and Richard Felter conducted an aerial survey of the range for the club. They determined that the best possible site for a new resort was a remote valley in the southern Sierra known as Mineral King.

The Forest Service, meanwhile, was also looking for new ski area possibilities, and it too was drawn to Mineral King. In mid-1949, the service issued a prospectus calling for bids "from individuals or firms who can show ability to develop and operate a resort and ski facility at Mineral King. . . ." The Forest Service prospectus called for a hotel accommodating at least 100 people, a mile-long chairlift, a 2,100-foot T-bar lift, and other features including "over-the-snow" transportation from Three Rivers to the valley—a tracked vehicle of some sort. The invitation called for bids from investors willing and able to spend at least $3 million on the resort.

The Sierra Club board, acting on the recommendations

Empire Mountain and Sawtooth Peak from a fractured granite ridge above Mineral King.

Vandever Mountain and White Chief Peak above Farewell Canyon, Mineral King. The forested slopes in the distance would have been criss-crossed with ski trails had the Disney resort been built.

Kaweah Peaks and Little Five Lakes, across the ridge from Mineral King in Sequoia National Park.

of its study team, resolved that the Club "finds no objection from the standpoint of its policies to the winter sports development in Mineral King as proposed by the U.S. Forest Service."

Despite the call by the Forest Service and the tepid endorsement by the Sierra Club, the Forest Service received not one bid in response to its prospectus. Interest remained in Mineral King as the site for a ski resort, but it would be some time before a package was put together that promised sufficient return to warrant the substantial investment necessary, particularly considering the difficult problem of access into the valley in winter. When a proposal that looked economically feasible eventually was presented to the Forest Service, it would bear little resemblance to the one suggested in 1949.

Quiet prevailed at Mineral King until 1961, when a young geologist from Bakersfield happened upon an intriguing rumor. Hiking in the basin over the Fourth of July weekend, he fell into conversation with a ranger who said he had heard that Walt Disney was planning a ski resort for the valley, with access to be provided by a monorail. Disney had visited Mineral King in the 1950s as a guest of one Ray Buckman, who owned land on the valley floor. Disney was also an avid fan of downhill skiing, having participated in the development of Sugar Bowl near Donner Summit (one of the two main peaks at Sugar Bowl is Mount Disney) and having helped stage the Winter Olympics at Squaw Valley in 1960. Following the Olympics, Disney had quietly asked the Forest Service if it was still interested in entertaining development proposals for Mineral King. The answer, though just as quiet, must have been yes.

Over the next several years, Disney employees studied the valley carefully for its ski potential. They also began secretly to buy out the owners of private property in and near the valley. (One of the companies that purchased an inholding from Ray Buckman was called "Retlaw"—Walter spelled backward.) At the same time, Sierra Club members, principal among whom was another young Bakersfield geologist named John Harper, gathered their own information on the geology of the valley, its flora and fauna. They aimed to assess the potential impact of a ski resort, not knowing for certain what was in the wind.

In February 1965 the Forest Service made it official. It published a prospectus and request for proposals. The prospectus described a resort with overnight accommodations for at least 100 people, trams or chairlifts capable of serving 2,000 people an hour, parking for 1,200 automobiles, sanitary and safety structures, and so forth. It was looking for a company or individual that would invest at least $3 million in the resort in addition to upgrading the access road to all-weather standards.

The Sierra Club took a look at the new prospectus and, after a rather rancorous year of internal argument, pronounced itself opposed to the project. It asked the Forest Service to withdraw the prospectus and convene public hearings on the matter.

The Forest Service was hardly pleased by this unexpected development. It replied that there had been a public hearing on the matter already—one chaired by local congressman Harlen Hagen in 1953, a dozen years earlier. Another hearing was not necessary. It was a thoroughly unsatisfactory answer,

and it was evident that the Forest Service had made up its mind to find a developer for Mineral King and was not at all interested in having a public debate on whether or not it was a good idea.

At this point the state of California got into the act, eliminating for a time one of the more difficult unresolved issues: who would pay the estimated $30 million to upgrade the road. On July 16, the state legislature incorporated the existing road into the state highway system and appropriated $3 million for preliminary construction. Further funds would be sought from the federal treasury.

On August 31, 1965, the Forest Service announced that it had received six bids for development of Mineral King, two of which were considered the leading candidates. One was from Robert Brandt, Beverly Hills film producer, investment banker, husband of the actress Janet Leigh, and well-connected Democrat. The other was from Walt Disney, a Republican and one of the best-loved people in the country.

Given the politics involved, Agriculture Secretary Orville Freeman wrested the decision-making power from local Forest Service officials and appointed a committee to advise him. In December, several months after the originally announced day of decision, and despite the fact that a Democratic administration was in power in Washington, Freeman announced that the Disney proposal had been accepted.

The Disney plan was decidedly ambitious. Where the Forest Service had called for an investment of $3 million, Disney planned to spend $35 million and proposed to build as many as twenty-seven chairlifts. The entire valley would be clogged with trams and lifts, ski jumps, sled runs, chalets and snack bars. Check dams up to twenty feet tall would be built on all the major creeks to keep debris from washing down to the valley floor. A notation that particularly disturbed conservationists read in part, "Considerable slope preparation [that is to say dynamite] will be required in the forested portions because of large boulders in some areas above an elevation of 8,000 feet. . . . Below timberline, trails of varying widths must be developed. . . ."

Disney also proposed two hotels and a dormitory to accommodate up to 3,000 overnight guests plus a thousand employees, a maximum ski-lift capacity of 11,400 per hour, ten restaurants and snack bars, a gas station, a theater, a chapel, a skating rink, and parking (in a ten-story, five-acre, underground garage below the valley itself) for 3,600 cars. All this, save the parking garage and service station, would be designed to look like a village in the Swiss Alps.

In short, Disney promised to build the world's greatest ski resort. It would be six times as big as Squaw Valley, the rival of Sun Valley, Aspen, and Chamonix. And that was just in winter. For summer visitors—who would actually comprise more than half the total each year—there would be fishing, hiking, tennis, golf, horseback riding, and swimming, in addition to camping in the backcountry of the national park, which could be easily reached by slinging one's backpack onto a chairlift or gondola.

Repeated pleas from the Sierra Club and others for a public

Glacially polished granite and the Kaweah River drainage, Sequoia National Park.

Lodgepole pine trunks, Sequoia National Park.

False hellebore in the Mineral King basin.

hearing on the project were denied or ignored. The Forest Service issued a formal three-year planning permit to Disney on October 10, 1966. Two months and five days later, Walt Disney died.

Attention then turned to the Department of the Interior. For the ski resort to become reality, the access road had to be widened, straightened, and paved to accommodate something over a thousand cars per hour. This was a daunting technical challenge and very expensive, estimated to cost in excess of a million dollars a mile. It also presented legal problems, in that eight miles of the road crossed Sequoia National Park.

When the Forest Service issued the planning permit to the Disney concern, the Park Service had not given permission for improvement of the road segment through the park. There was a matter of principle involved—allowing the building of roads through national parks simply to get to the other side was generally forbidden—and also the prospect that a new road would carve massive gashes up the valley of the East Fork of the Kaweah and unavoidably threaten hundreds of giant sequoias.

Interior Secretary Stewart Udall was distinctly cool to the whole idea of developing the valley. It was his firm belief that Mineral King was logically and ecologically a part of the national park, and that it was no place for a giant commercial development. Udall stonewalled the Forest Service and the state for more than a year, but he was fighting a losing battle. California wanted the resort, the Agriculture Department wanted the resort, and Udall had some political debts to pay.

As President Johnson's administration drew to a close, there were three major national conservation struggles to be resolved, and all three had the Interior Department and the Agriculture Department pulling in opposite directions. One was Mineral King. A second was the effort to create the North Cascades National Park in Washington State. The third was the campaign to create a Redwood National Park in northern California. For both national park proposals, the Forest Service would have to relinquish some of its holdings, turning them over to the Park Service. (In the redwoods, the Park Service would then trade the Forest Service lands for private lands nearby.)

In California, an additional factor was that much of the land proposed for the Redwood National Park was already in state parks. Governor Reagan was cool to the park proposal, but he was a strong proponent of the ski resort in Mineral King. Eventually, to pay Orville Freeman back for some favors in the Cascades and the Redwoods, to buy the cooperation of Ronald Reagan, and to lighten the pressure being heaped on his shoulders by the Bureau of the Budget, Udall quietly gave in: on December 26, 1967, the Bureau of the Budget announced that the state would get its right-of-way through Sequoia National Park. Udall delayed formally approving the right-of-way until the following November, when he gave preliminary approval. The last possible block in the way of the project had been removed. There was nowhere else to turn.

Nowhere, that is, except to the courts. On December 14, 1968, the Board of Directors of the Sierra Club authorized the filing of a lawsuit to prevent the development of Mineral King.

Until the middle 1960s, the federal courts had firmly rebuffed attempts by conservationists to bring cases to court to protect natural resources. In order to establish the necessary "standing to sue," the courts held that injury to financial interests had to be demonstrated. But in 1965, the United States Court of Appeals for the Second Circuit in New York found that in certain circumstances an "aesthetic, conservational, or recreational" interest could suffice to establish standing. The case involved a proposed reservoir at Storm King Mountain on the Hudson River. The Sierra Club had participated in that litigation as a friend of the court. Lawyers on the Sierra Club Legal Committee, an all-volunteer body that assisted the Club with legal affairs, had noted the decision with interest at the time and begun to mull over the possibility of taking advantage of it in pursuit of other conservation objectives.

Following the board's December resolution on Mineral King, Michael McCloskey, the Sierra Club's conservation director, approached a young attorney named Robert Jasperson of the Conservation Law Society of America, a nonprofit adjunct of a commercial law firm upstairs from the Club's offices in downtown San Francisco. The Society was the brainchild of long-time Club director Richard M. Leonard, who had established it to provide low-cost legal services to conservation organizations. Jasperson was its only employee. McCloskey asked him to take a look at the Mineral King dispute and see if there were any ways the project might be attacked through litigation.

Jasperson and another lawyer, Greg Archbald, researched the matter and suggested that the Mineral King project was illegal in at least three respects. First, there were Forest Service regulations in force that limited the size and duration of leases the agency was allowed to give to private concerns: thirty-year leases could cover no more than eighty acres. The Forest Service was skirting this problem by saying it would give Disney a thirty-year lease for the eighty acres the hotels and other permanent structures would occupy. The rest of the necessary acreage—which would run into the thousands of acres for ski runs—would be committed via one-year, revocable leases. This, Jasperson and Archbald suggested, was a patent attempt to make an end run around the eighty-acre limitation.

A second possible "cause of action" would be against the Park Service, whose regulations require that roads in national parks be simple, narrow, and built solely for the convenience of visitors to the park. Roads are not to be allowed if they are meant only to convey people from one side of a park to the other. The Mineral King road surely fit that description.

Finally, a major resort development was clearly incompatible with the purposes of a national game refuge, set aside explicitly to provide protection and sanctuary for deer and other creatures that might not mingle well with upwards of 14,000 people a day.

Jasperson and Archbald gave their report to McCloskey. He then turned to the Legal Committee, whose chairman was another young attorney, Philip Berry of Oakland. Berry had

Kaweah Peaks reflect in a frozen lake.
This part of Sequoia National Park
would have been inundated by hikers
and campers arriving via ski lift
from just across the ridge.

been pushing the Sierra Club to think creatively about using the law in the service of conservation since he was appointed chairman of the committee in 1966. He had recruited Fred Fisher, a friend from Stanford Law School, who had brought in Don Harris, one of his partners at the San Francisco firm Lillick, McHose, Wheat, Adams & Charles. Harris, an avid fisherman, had been active in Trout Unlimited, an organization of anglers active in conservation, particularly of streams. The two men soon became the backbone of the legal committee.

Fisher and Harris studied the Mineral King report and determined that it contained the seeds of a worthwhile lawsuit. Neither man had time to take on the case just then, being already embroiled in other legal matters on the Club's behalf. They enlisted the services of the firm Feldman, Waldman & Kline, which had offices across the street from the Sierra Club. Leo Borregard, Matthew Mitchell, and Leland J. Selna set to building the case. Selna took the lead.

The Disney team handed its master plan to the Forest Service on January 8, 1969. On January 18, in the waning hours of his tenure as Interior Secretary, Stewart Udall issued new road-building rules for the Park Service. Under the new rules, the Park Service could not approve any road through a national park without first holding public hearings on both the route and the design of the proposed road. Richard Nixon took the oath of office on January 20, and the next day the Forest Service announced its formal approval of the Disney master plan in language redolent of Madison Avenue:

> On the site of the old, decaying mining town of Mineral King will rise a new self-contained village bearing the same name. Imaginative in concept and contemporary in design, this carefully planned development will create one of the world's major outdoor recreation facilities in a spectacular valley of the California Sierras [sic]. Free of cars and skillfully blended into the alpine setting, Mineral King and its attractions will provide wholesome enjoyment for thousands of American families.

On February 24, an avalanche thundered down a slope into the valley, flattening several buildings and killing a Disney employee within a few yards of the spot where Disney planned to build its alpine village. On April 21, Walter Hickel of Alaska, who replaced Udall as Secretary of the Interior, revoked Udall's January 18 road rules. Formal granting of the right-of-way was thought to be imminent.

Lee Selna filed suit in the U.S. District Court for the Northern District of California in San Francisco on June 5, 1969. The case was assigned to Judge William T. Sweigert, a protégé and political ally of Earl Warren, former governor of California and later Chief Justice of the United States. Sweigert had no record in environmental matters, though he was known as something of a maverick, having once ruled that the Vietnam War was unconstitutional.

Selna asked the court to issue an injunction that would block the Forest Service and Park Service from allowing any work on the resort or the road realignment to commence until the merits of the Club's case could be determined by a trial. Those claims were refinements of the theories propounded by Bob Jasperson and Greg Archbald: that the road was illegal, that the leases were illegal, and that the resort would violate the game refuge. Selna argued that an injunction was necessary, because if work were allowed to begin, any damage incurred would be irreparable. The case, however, was never to be tried on its merits; what would occupy the courts and the lawyers for many months to come was the critical issue of standing to sue.

In its brief to the trial court, the Sierra Club had argued that it should be granted standing simply because its very purpose for existence was the preservation of the Sierra Nevada. "If the Sierra Club may not be heard," the plaintiff asked rhetorically, "then who speaks for the future generations for whose benefit Congress intended the fragile Sierra bowls and valleys to be preserved? If the Sierra Club does not have standing, then who may question the threatened illegal acts of the secretaries to whom this unique and irreplaceable natural resource has been entrusted? Who may challenge their breach of trust when they sell for money government land which is literally priceless in aid of a project for private profit?"

It was a moving and eloquent statement, and it quite persuaded Judge Sweigert. Nowhere, however, did the Club claim that its interest as an organization or the interests of its members would be harmed by the Mineral King development. The Club was trying for a far broader affirmation of standing—that it had a right to bring suit to defend public lands simply because one of its principal purposes as an organization was precisely to defend public lands. Whether the Club had overreached its grasp is the question that would be thrashed out over the next three years.

Here we must back up two years to pick up another thread of the story. In 1967, in Washington, D.C., three young lawyers had set out to create an organization that would represent the unrepresented, fight for the underdog, and not charge for its services: a public-interest law firm, in other words, supported mainly by foundations. Their names were Charles Halpern, Bruce Terris, and Geoffrey Cowan. Terris's passion was consumer law. Halpern's was health, mainly mental health. Cowan was interested in communications law. To round out the services offered by their firm they wanted a lawyer to specialize in the environment.

They asked Eddie Weinberg, the former Solicitor of the Interior Department, if he could recommend anyone. The Solicitor—the department's in-house lawyer—handles some of the agency's legal work; major lawsuits are usually defended by lawyers from the Department of Justice. Weinberg had recently been involved in a legal proceeding in California having to do with access to federal water for irrigation, and he had

Krummholz juniper near Pinto Lake, Sequoia National Park.

been much impressed with the performance of a young lawyer from the Lands Division of the Justice Department. His name was James Moorman. (His full name was James Watt Moorman, but the middle name didn't provoke jokes until Ronald Reagan appointed his first Secretary of the Interior a dozen years later.) Weinberg knew that Moorman was looking for something to do once the Nixon administration took office and thought he might fit well into this new enterprise. Moorman took the job with the Center for Law and Social Policy.

In the next two and a half years Moorman and the Center were to bring many important environmental cases representing a number of the leading national environmental groups. The two most famous were one that forced the Environmental Protection Agency to take the pesticide DDT off the market and another that delayed construction of the trans-Alaska pipeline for five years. Moorman found that public-interest environmental law suited him well; soon he would team up with Don Harris, Fred Fisher, and Phil Berry to create a public-interest law firm devoted exclusively to environmental litigation.

Judge Sweigert was not at all bothered by the Club's broad claim to standing, and he also thought the Club had a strong case. On July 23, 1969, he issued a preliminary injunction halting all further work on the project, pending trial. The bold stroke had paid off, at least for a time. The story ran in all major newspapers and elicited editorial comment in many of them. Reporters and editors were intrigued both by the battle over Mineral King and by the relative novelty of involving the court in such a fight.

The injunction forced the Forest Service, and the Justice Department defending it, to make a strategic choice. Should they continue to fight the case before Judge Sweigert, who had left little doubt that he considered the Sierra Club's objections to the development sound and well grounded in the law and in federal regulations, and then appeal an adverse decision? Or should they go straight to the Court of Appeals — through a device known as an interlocutory appeal — and ask that court to overrule Judge Sweigert on the procedural question of the Sierra Club's standing to bring the case in the first place?

The defendants chose the latter course and five months later — on December 29, 1969 — challenged the plaintiff's standing before the Ninth Circuit Court of Appeals in San Francisco, asking the court to lift the injunction and allow the project to go forward.

Disney, meanwhile, sensing that it was losing the contest for public opinion, dressed its window with a handful of men who it hoped would add new respectability to its Mineral King project — a conservation advisory committee to ensure that environmental planning was carried out with "sensitivity." Committee members included a former director of the National Park Service, the Executive Director of the National Wildlife Federation, and a former president of the Sierra Club. Their influence did not change the outcome of the struggle, but the technique of enlisting possible adversaries on one side of a public battle was to be used frequently in future environmental conflicts.

Briefing the Court of Appeals took six weeks and oral argument was held on February 9, 1970. Seven months later, on September 17, the Court of Appeals, by a vote of two to one, overruled Judge Sweigert and dissolved the injunction.

The court went systematically through the case. First, it found that the Sierra Club had not claimed a substantial enough interest in the dispute to warrant its bringing the case at all — in other words, it had no standing to sue. "The proposed course of action [the ski resort] does not please the Club's officers and directors and through them all or a substantial number of its members. It would prefer some other type of action or none at all. . . . We do not believe such Club concern without a showing of more direct interest can constitute standing in the legal sense." The Court then rejected all the Sierra Club's legal arguments — against the size and duration of the leases, against the road right-of-way, against the misuse of a game refuge.

Fortunately for the Sierra Club, however, the Court of Appeals had not been asked to review the merits of the case but only whether the Sierra Club had standing and whether the injunction issued by Judge Sweigert was proper. The Club immediately announced that it would ask the U.S. Supreme Court to review the decision of the Court of Appeals, and on October 6 the Appeals Court agreed to leave the injunction in place until the Supreme Court could be heard from. Briefs were filed by the various parties — Tulare County and the Far West Ski Association had by now weighed in on the side of the ski resort — and the high court announced on February 22, 1971, that it would review the case.

The Disney organization, incidentally, never became a party to the legal battle over its proposed resort, preferring to stay above the fray. The Disney attitude seemed to be that while it would build this resort as a service to the country, its government, and its citizens, it was not begging to do so and would not stoop to fighting over the project in the courts. Disney's public statements throughout the long battle tended to be restrained and sober. In fact, its spokesmen insisted that they favored allowing the Club's legal challenge to be tested in court. As Disney project manager Robert Hicks said to the California State Chamber of Commerce in Los Angeles on January 15, 1970, "Citizens should have a place to go to test arbitrary and capricious agency actions. The judiciary affords a safety valve which in my judgment is pretty vital to the preservation of this tripartite system of government. This is not all bad, even on my side of the fence. The Sierra Club is doing a lot of people a favor, since these streets must run both ways."

Just as the county and the skiers had entered the arena on the side of the development, three environmental organizations had chimed in on the side of the Sierra Club. Jim Moorman and Bruce Terris of the Center for Law and Social Policy, writing on behalf of The Wilderness Society, Friends of the Earth, and the Izaak Walton League of America, did what the Sierra Club had declined to do: they recited at great length the Sierra Club's historic and specific interest in Mineral King—the use of Mineral King by the Sierra Club as an organization, the use of Mineral King by individual Sierra Club members for recreational purposes, and the injury both the Club and its members would suffer if the resort were built.

By this time, Don Harris and Fred Fisher had applied to the Ford Foundation for a grant to establish the Sierra Club Legal Defense Fund. In order to qualify for tax-deductible support, the new organization was kept wholly independent of the Sierra Club, which had lost its own tax-deductible status a few years earlier. In the spring of 1971 Ford awarded a grant of $98,000 to support the Legal Defense Fund for two years. The board was made up principally of lawyers. In May their first meeting was held at Don Harris's home in Berkeley.

Harris was elected president, Fisher vice president. They then embarked on a search for an executive director for the Legal Defense Fund. They knew of Jim Moorman through his suit against the trans-Alaska pipeline. Moorman had heard about the new organization from Beatrice Laws, who worked for the legal committee. Moorman telephoned Harris and Fisher, and they invited him out for an interview. The three men liked each other immediately. Moorman accepted the job, and agreed to begin work in August.

In the meantime, Supreme Court arguments were being prepared in the Mineral King case. Moorman appealed to Lee Selna to embrace the standing arguments he had articulated in the friend of the court briefs, but to no avail. Selna was firmly committed to the original approach, arguing in favor of a broad concept of standing to sue.

Oral arguments were scheduled and then postponed. Justices Hugo L. Black and John M. Harlan had retired from the Court at the end of its term in the spring of 1971, and both seats remained open when the court reconvened in the fall of that year. On November 17, 1971, at 11:06 A.M., the court sat to hear the arguments in the Mineral King case.

In his opening argument, Selna tried to establish the Club's right to standing. "As an incident of the Club's interest in the area, some of its members use Mineral King," he said.

"Does the record show that?" asked Justice Blackmun, who was in fact sympathetic to the Club's position.

"The record contains a letter which is written by a member of the Board of Directors of the Sierra Club, in which he in turn refers to his trips to Mineral King," Selna replied.

"But there isn't any direct testimony by members of the Club anywhere in the record, is there?" Blackmun continued.

"Direct testimony concerning their use, Mr. Justice Blackmun? No there is not."

Justice Potter Stewart was skeptical:

"I was just wondering how far your argument would go. I'm reminded of these so-called clubs that get chartered airplane flights across the Atlantic Ocean, these ad hoc organizations. Could I form a club, Friends of Walt Disney Productions, and come in on the other side as a party?" (Selna thought not.)

Chief Justice Burger wanted to know if John Muir could be a party to the case as an individual. (Selna thought he could.)

Justice Blackmun tried again to help. "If an organization like the Sierra Club is not qualified to bring litigation of this kind, who would be?"

"Nobody," Selna answered.

Erwin N. Griswold, Solicitor of the United States, represented the government. He called the case "the ultimate case on standing. If the petitioner here has standing, then I believe it's fair to conclude that anyone who asserts an interest in a controversy has standing."

Griswold went on, "Should judges be dealing almost continuously with heated social and economic controversies? Will not the courts be in a better position to decide the many difficult and important questions which only the courts can effectively resolve in our constitutional system if they do not undertake to decide all the legal questions that anyone—anyone—wants to present to them?"

In his rebuttal, Selna insisted that finding in favor of the Sierra Club would not throw the court open to cases by "anyone."

"It should be clear from our argument that we do not urge that the doors of the courts be opened wide to anyone. We've argued that there are criteria that should be applied by a court, by which organizations' or individuals' qualifications for standing should be tested.

"The Club in this case did, in fact, allege its special interest in the area involved, and no one in California, at the District Court level, had any question in their mind as to the deep involvement of the Club with Sequoia National Park and Mineral King."

At 1:15 P.M. Chief Justice Burger gaveled the hearing to a close.

Christopher D. Stone, a law professor at the University of Southern California, had followed the case with interest, and he wanted to add a twist he had been working out for some time. Whereas one could argue about whether the Sierra Club or its members would be "injured" by the defiling of Mineral King, no one could deny that the valley itself would be injured. Why not, then, provide legal standing to natural objects themselves, with the courts empowered to appoint attorneys to represent their interests in the same way that governments provide lawyers for people unable to afford their own private counsel?

As it happened, the spring 1972 issue of the *University of Southern California Law Review* was to carry a special symposium on law and technology, for which Supreme Court Justice William O. Douglas had agreed to write a preface. Stone persuaded the editor to make room for a last-minute article, and then whipped it into shape. It was titled "Should Trees Have Standing?" A draft of the article was sent to Justice

Upper Mosquito Lake, Sequoia National Park. Proposed ski lifts would have cut through the Mosquito Lakes chain.

Douglas in late October or early November.

The Supreme Court issued its ruling in *Sierra Club* v. *Morton* on April 19, 1972. By a vote of four to three (Burger, Stewart, Marshall, and White in the majority; Blackmun, Brennan, and Douglas in the minority) the Court sustained the Court of Appeals, dissolved the injunction, and ruled that the Sierra Club did not have standing to sue. It was clear, however, that the Court majority simply felt that the Club had tried to reach just a little too far, that its claim to standing was a bit too broad. The Club, in short, had failed to allege that it or its members would be injured by the development of Mineral King. "Nowhere in the pleadings or affidavits," Justice Stewart wrote, "did the Club state that its members use Mineral King for any purpose, much less that they use it in any way that would be significantly affected by the proposed actions of the respondents."

Stewart then dropped the broadest possible hint, in one of the most famous footnotes in environmental jurisprudence: "Our decision does not, of course, bar the Sierra Club from seeking in the District Court to amend its complaint."

Which is precisely what the Sierra Club did.

Before we leave the Supreme Court, however, it is interesting to look briefly at the dissenting opinions which, in a curious way, got rolled together with the majority opinion in a new and much broadened definition of standing in environmental law. Justice Blackmun wrote, "The case poses—if only we choose to acknowledge and reach them—significant aspects of a wide, growing, and disturbing problem, that is, the Nation's and the world's deteriorating environment with its resulting ecological disturbances. Must our law be so rigid and our procedural concepts so inflexible that we render ourselves helpless when the existing methods and the traditional concepts . . . do not prove to be entirely adequate for new issues?"

Then, expanding on Christopher Stone's notion of standing, Justice Douglas contributed his celebrated dissent:

> The critical question of "standing" would be simplified and also put neatly in focus if we fashioned a federal rule that allowed environmental issues to be litigated before federal agencies or federal courts in the name of the inanimate object about to be despoiled, defaced, or invaded by roads and bulldozers and where injury is the subject of public outrage. Contemporary public concern for protecting nature's ecological equilibrium should lead to the conferral of standing upon environmental objects to sue for their own preservation. . . . This suit would therefore be more properly labeled as *Mineral King* v. *Morton.*

It was a massive victory, disguised as a defeat. The press reflected the confusion. "Sierra Club Loses on Mineral King" said the headline in the *San Francisco Examiner.* "A heavy blow" said *The New York Times.* "A temporary defeat," thought the *Wall Street Journal.* "Mineral King Setback for Sierra Club" headlined the *San Francisco Chronicle.* But *Time* magazine, which had a few days to think it over, called the decision "an important victory" for conservationists.

On June 2, the Sierra Club, represented now by Jim Moorman and the Sierra Club Legal Defense Fund, marched back into Judge Sweigert's courtroom and asked for permission to amend its suit. The revised complaint had several new features. It described in considerable detail the Sierra Club's interests in Mineral King and how those interests would be injured by the Disney project. To be safe, it added as plaintiffs nine individuals who visited Mineral King frequently, plus the Mineral King District Association, a group whose members owned property in and near the valley.

And, in what proved to be the *coup de grâce,* it added a new claim under the National Environmental Policy Act, which had been enacted after the original suit was filed. The Act orders federal agencies to prepare an environmental impact statement for "major federal actions significantly affecting the quality of the human environment." Moorman asked the court to order the government to prepare such a statement on the resort and requested that the injunction be reinstated until the impact statement was completed and a trial could be held on the allegations in the original suit.

The government argued that the case should be dismissed because the Court of Appeals had already rejected it on its merits, even though the majority opinion from the Supreme Court had said specifically, "we intimate no view on the merits of the complaint." Judge Sweigert, who was still irked at having his reasoning spurned by two higher courts, rejected the government's plea, noting that the new claim under NEPA was enough to reinstate the case and reimpose the injunction.

Ironically, it now seems clear that the way the Sierra Club argued its case for standing in its original suit was a tactical error—it did lose in the Supreme Court, after all—but a strategic success. By the same reasoning, the government's challenge to the Club's standing was a tactical success and a strategic disaster: if the government had declined to challenge the Club's standing, Judge Sweigert's likely ruling in the Club's favor on the merits of the case would almost certainly have been reversed by the Court of Appeals. And since such a decision would not have considered the issue of standing to sue, it is highly unlikely that the Sierra Club could have persuaded the Supreme Court to review the case. No one can say what would have happened, of course, but the consensus is that if the government hadn't challenged the Club's standing in the Court of Appeals, there would very likely be a ski resort in Mineral King valley today.

The political battle over Mineral King was to drag on for several years, but the legal campaign was all but over. Lawyers for the Legal Defense Fund prepared to go to trial, questioned Forest Service and Park Service employees, and counseled Club members and others who were participating in the environmental impact statement-writing process.

The draft environmental impact statement was issued on January 3, 1975. Four thousand four hundred individuals, fourteen federal agencies, six state agencies, seven local government agencies, and thirty-five private organizations filed comments on the draft, many of them scathing. The California

Kaweah Peaks and the Great Western Divide, Sequoia National Park.

Department of Fish and Game worried about the impact of the resort on wildlife. The Interior Department retained reservations about the impact on Sequoia National Park. Public comments were overwhelmingly anti-resort.

By 1975 Mineral King was one of the most prominent national environmental issues. All major national organizations had endorsed the idea of adding the valley to Sequoia National Park, and legislation to accomplish the transfer was rapidly gaining supporters. The Forest Service was still firmly committed to the project, but the Disney organization was growing weary of the fight and uneasy as public opposition to the resort steadily grew.

And there was still the matter of the road. Disney had always insisted that it would not pay the cost of improving the road to all-weather standards. The federal government had never agreed to undertake the project itself, and in August 1972 the state of California rescinded its earlier pledge to pay for it. In signing the bill that took the access road out of the state highway system, Governor Reagan insisted that he still supported the resort, but that it was improper for the state to pay for highway improvements. Disney had proposed some months earlier a cog-assisted railroad into the valley, and now suggested that Tulare County could raise the necessary $20 million with a bond issue.

The final environmental impact statement was released by the Forest Service in February 1976. The project by that time had shrunk considerably. Daily visitation was down from 14,000 to 8,000 in winter and 6,000 in summer. The capacity of the parking lot had dropped from 3,600 to 2,200 (the cog-railway plan had quickly come a cropper). No longer were there to be ski-lift towers on the boundaries of the national park. All ski activity, in fact, would take place in the bowls on the west and south sides of the valley, well away from the back

packers' trails into the Sequoia backcountry. Oddly, despite the reduced size of the project, the price tag had remained at roughly $35 million, which raised questions about how Disney expected to turn a profit with just over half of the customers it had originally anticipated. A visit to the alpine Disneyland was looking like a rather expensive outing.

The legal effort on behalf of Mineral King came to an end on March 11, 1977. Judge Sweigert was preparing to retire from the bench, and since the case had lain dormant on his desk for four and a half years, he dismissed it himself for "lack of prosecution." The judge's order left the Sierra Club the opportunity to resurrect the case if that became necessary, but in fact the case was closed. An attempt to revive the project was made at the beginning of the Carter administration, but it went nowhere.

In October 1978, as part of a monumental national parks acquisition and expansion bill guided through Congress by Representative Phillip Burton of San Francisco, Mineral King was added to Sequoia National Park, where it belonged from the start.

When the Sierra Club decided actively to oppose the Disney ski resort, it was bucking very long odds. The state's governor favored the project, as did the state legislature, the state highway commission, the state's major newspapers, the President of the United States, the Secretary of Agriculture, local congressmen, and both California senators. By 1978 all that had changed. Litigation bought time for the political process to work. The same litigation established forever that environmental concerns had a right to the protection of the legal system.

Admiralty Island
Wilderness, Logging, and the Sitka Black-tailed Deer

I n October 1882, the U.S. Navy attacked the tiny Tlingit village of Angoon on the western shore of Admiralty Island in southeast Alaska. Gunfire from boats offshore leveled all but four buildings. Smoke from fires set by the shelling suffocated six children. When the dust settled, sailors and marines came ashore and hacked forty dugout canoes to kindling. Some say that treatment of the town and its inhabitants by outsiders hasn't improved markedly since then.

The Tlingits settled "Southeast" soon after the ice sheets of the most recent ice age receded, leaving the tangled web of fjords, passages, bays, inlets, islands, mountains, and valleys now known as the Alaska panhandle. They established communities that depended mainly on salmon, halibut, and other fish in summer, deer and smoked fish in winter, berries in the spring, shellfish and seaweed the year round. They evolved a culture and society closely in tune with the rhythms of the land around them. They carved totem poles to tell stories and preserve knowledge. Their name for themselves means "those whose table is set when the tide is out."

Seymour Canal and the Glass Peninsula, Admiralty Island National Monument, Alaska.

Forested slopes of Admiralty Island from the air.

Alaskan brown bear (Ursus arctos), *Admiralty Island. By Art Wolfe.*

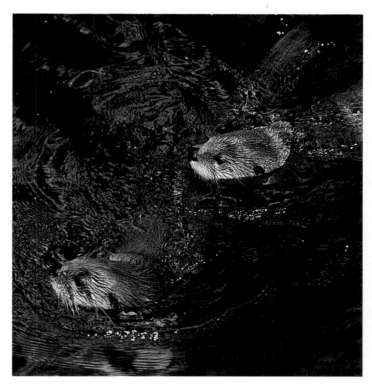

River otters (Lutra canadensis). *By C. Allan Morgan/Peter Arnold, Inc.*

In 1741 Russian explorers became the first Europeans to set foot in Southeast, claiming it for the motherland. The Russians built small settlements and recruited Tlingits to the Orthodox church. They trapped fur-bearing animals and caught large quantities of fish. The English Navy captain George Vancouver explored the area in 1794, visiting a large island just offshore from where Juneau now sits. This was the island on which the village of Angoon was situated; Vancouver named it Admiralty Island in honor of the British Admiralty.

The Tlingit already had a name for the island. They called it Kootznoowoo, the fortress of the bears. Just how invincible this fortress would turn out to be is the subject of the present narrative. Of the bears there can be no question. More than a thousand Alaskan brown bears—grizzlies—live there, the densest concentration anywhere in the world.

Admiralty is a hundred miles long and averages twenty-five miles wide. It covers a little more than a million acres. A spine of peaks marches the length of the island, with a gap about midway along that has allowed latter-day adventurers to establish a canoe-and-portage route from one side to the other.

As with neighboring lands, the lowlands are heavily forested down to the high-tide line on the coast and the high-water mark on lakes and streams. Occasional muskeg openings (muskeg is a freshwater wetland dominated by sphagnum moss) break the fastness of the forest, and wide grassy mudflats provide relief where rivers enter the myriad bays. But up to about 2,500 feet elevation, forest is king, there giving way to upland meadows and, at still higher elevations, to granite, snow, and ice.

In addition to the bears, terrestrial animals on Admiralty include otter, marten, beaver, marmot, snowshoe hare, and several species of vole. Large herds of Sitka black-tailed deer—a principal player in this story—summer in the high country and winter in the lowland forest, and five species of salmon spawn in Admiralty's sixty-seven salmon streams. Admiralty is as thick with bald eagles as it is with bears: as many as 2,760 pairs nest in big old spruces and hemlocks near the coast, the densest year-round concentration of the species in the world. (It is intriguing to speculate on how many bald eagles once filled Admiralty's skies; a bounty was paid for the birds until 1952, and in the forty-one years before the bounty was lifted, hunters collected fees for killing 128,273 of our national birds.)

Humpback and killer whales cruise the waters off Admiralty, and often seek shelter from storms in its bays and inlets. Great blue herons and dozens more species of wading birds stalk the grassy flats. Blueberries, salmonberries, and other delicacies abound on the forest floor. In all, at least 150 species of ducks, shorebirds, songbirds, and raptors visit the island at least part of the year.

In the last century several canneries for salmon (and one "saltery" for herring), a whaling station, and an establishment called the Alaska Oil and Guano Company were built and operated on Admiralty. Sportsmen constructed a handful of cabins for fishing and hunting. All but the cabins and one lodge for sportsmen and sightseers have vanished, leaving Angoon the only settlement on the island. By the mid-1960s, time had healed most of the scars left by earlier human endeavors.

That Admiralty remained relatively pristine is something of a miracle. If the U.S. Forest Service had had its way, every stick of salable timber on the island would eventually have been cut, pulped, and shipped abroad, leaving behind only

Barnacle-encrusted rocks, the Glass Peninsula, Admiralty Island.

Weathered fishing boats in Favorite Bay, Admiralty Island.

Old-growth spruce and hemlock forest, west coast of Admiralty Island. These are the trees that were at the center of the logging controversy.

devastation. The fight for Admiralty would eventually rage for nearly twenty years and be a major preoccupation of conservationists inside and outside Alaska. It would be one of the Legal Defense Fund's longest, most complex campaigns.

The United States purchased Alaska from Russia in 1867. The Tongass National Forest was created in 1902; it now encompasses nearly all of southeast Alaska and, at sixteen million acres, is three times the size of the second biggest national forest (the Chugach, also in Alaska). Admiralty was added to the Tongass in 1909. In 1901, President Theodore Roosevelt suggested creating a bear sanctuary on Admiralty and nearby Baranof and Chichagof islands, but to no avail. Later suggestions for making Admiralty a national park or national monument likewise were foiled, mainly by interests that hoped to cash in on the natural resources of the island.

Ever since the 1920s, the Forest Service has had as its mission the creation of an economy based on timber in southeast Alaska. As early as 1927 the Forest Service published a prospectus and advertised for bids on two major timber sales on the Tongass, but the remoteness of the area, the high cost of moving logs from forest to mill, and the availability of cheaper timber elsewhere combined to discourage any likely bidders.

The Forest Service can be patient, however. As other industries went into decline (the salmon catch in Southeast hit a peak of 256 million pounds in 1941; a decade later it was 8 million), it revived its efforts to promote a timber industry in the region.

In 1947 Congress expressed itself on the subject, passing the Tongass Timber Act, which specifically authorized the sale of timber from the forest, giant spruces that yield wood prized for making guitar sounding boards and smaller, knottier cedar and hemlock usable primarily for pulp. The Forest Service divided the forest into three parts: the Ketchikan Unit, in the southern third of the forest; the Juneau Unit, which includes Admiralty and two areas on the mainland; and the Sitka Unit, which contains large portions of Baranof and Chichagof islands, to the west of Admiralty. Each of the first two units was thought to contain in excess of 8 billion board feet of salable timber, the third unit approximately 5 billion board feet (a board foot being a piece of wood a foot long, a foot wide, and an inch thick).

When many Forest Service planners look at a forest like the Tongass, they do so with contempt. The Tongass National Forest, like other temperate-zone climax forests, is officially classified as "overmature," which means that it is not increasing in volume from year to year and may actually decline in some years. To someone who wants to harvest as much wood fiber as possible from a piece of land, this is painful. As a 1973 report from the Forest Service said—and this is typical—"These mature and overmature stands should be harvested as rapidly as possible since their volumes will not increase in years to come." The Forest Service, in the matter at hand, was not talking about selected pruning of these decadent, senior-citizen trees: it was talking about clearcutting the entire Tongass National

Forest. For at least the past fifty years, the Forest Service's official policy has been the "liquidation" of old-growth forest in Southeast to encourage faster production of wood fiber.

Another passage from that 1973 report is typical of how the agency justifies its policy. Under the heading of "Favorable Environmental Impacts" appear the following "benefits":

> The forest will have on the cutover blocks twice the timber volume after 100 years [this may be an economic benefit; it is hardly an environmental one].
>
> There will be a permanent road system [ditto].
>
> There will be less loss to insects and disease [this is far from a certainty].
>
> There will be openings that benefit certain wildlife species [and harm others].
>
> There will be roads that make fish habitat improvement programs possible in otherwise unaccessible places [but it's the roads that damage the habitat in the first place].
>
> Cutting along streams *may* [emphasis added] raise temperatures to more optimum [whatever that means] levels [for what isn't stated].

With benefits like these, one hardly needs costs. As of 1947, ecological realities were little understood, little heeded. The Forest Service saw its responsibility as providing wood fiber and jobs; all other concerns were secondary.

Encouraged by Congress, the Forest Service again offered the timber in the Ketchikan Unit for sale, and after protracted negotiations the sale was made in 1951 to the Ketchikan Pulp Company. The Chief of the Forest Service hailed the sale as "the realization of a hope which the U.S. Forest Service has cherished for almost fifty years." The Sitka Unit timber was later sold to the Alaska Lumber and Pulp Company, which is now wholly owned by a company in Japan.

The Juneau Unit—containing Admiralty—was first offered for sale in the mid-1950s, and an option was taken by Georgia Pacific. The company never cut a tree, however, deciding that the deal wasn't economical after all, and withdrew from the sale.

Ten years later, the Forest Service found another buyer, the St. Regis Paper Company. St. Regis offered to buy 8.75 billion board feet of timber over a period of fifty years, paying the Forest Service approximately five dollars per thousand board feet for the wood. It would build a combination pulp and lumber mill near the areas to be logged; the Forest Service would build the roads. It was the biggest timber deal ever struck by the Forest Service. But again, something about the deal didn't feel right to the company and St. Regis pulled out. This time, however, the respite was not very long.

U.S. Plywood had been the second highest bidder after St. Regis, and the Forest Service asked Plywood officials if they would like to take over the deal. Three years had passed and the price of timber had inflated considerably, but the agency didn't have the forest reevaluated; it offered the sale on the same terms it had made with St. Regis. U.S. Plywood agreed, and on September 12, 1968, a contract was signed with much fanfare in Juneau.

Businessmen in Juneau were delighted. The town's gold mine had shut down during World War II and not reopened. Alaska's citizens had just voted to build a brand new state capital between Anchorage and Fairbanks, depriving Juneau of its major economic base. (This decision was reversed years later; Juneau is still the state's capital.) The new mill was just what the city thought it needed for an economic renaissance.

There were some in Juneau, however, who saw the imminent logging and mill as a catastrophe in the making. One was Karl Lane, a guide who had been taking people to Admiralty for many years to hunt, fish, and take photographs. He and other guides and writers, notably Ralph Young, Frank Dufresne, and Corey Ford, had been agitating for ten years in the pages of *Field and Stream* and elsewhere about protection for Admiralty. They knew full well what the Forest Service had in store for the island. They also had seen what a relatively small timber sale in 1963 had done to Whitewater Bay, south of Angoon, silting in the salmon streams, leaving raw scars and ruined habitat.

Timber interests like to talk about nature's power of regeneration, but they often leave out key details. It's not that the forest won't spring back once it's cut. It springs back almost too fast. Once land is cleared, alders grow so dense and so fast that entering the forest is physically impossible for all but the smallest creatures. Biologists reckon that clearcut land in that part of the world will take at least 100 years and perhaps twice that long to regain its ability to support wildlife.

One of the concerned parties was Cliff Lobaugh, the only veterinarian in that part of Southeast at the time, who commuted by float plane from town to town, ministering to ailing animals. Lobaugh had a cabin on the northern part of Admiralty where he went to hunt and relax. Another was Rich Gordon, a biologist who worked as a librarian for the state's Department of Fish and Game. And there was Dick Myron, a fisheries biologist who studied salmon for the National Marine Fisheries Service. They, along with several others, formed the Stellar Society to fend off what they saw as Armageddon for their beloved island wilderness.

Rich Gordon decided to try to enlist the support of Territorial Sportsmen, a powerful group of hunters and fishermen. Sportsmen then as now wielded considerable influence in Alaska, and Gordon hoped to win their support for "The Wild Forest of Admiralty," an informal designation based on the rules that governed the Boundary Waters Canoe Area in Minnesota —not as restricted as wilderness, but nearly so. Creation of the Wild Forest of Admiralty would clearly preclude logging on the scale the Forest Service planned. Hunters and fishermen ought, by rights, to be sympathetic to a proposal that would save some of their most cherished spots from clearcutting. The Territorial Sportsmen adopted the plan in an open meeting, but members of their board asked permission to present it to the Forest Service privately before any public announcement. The plan was suppressed—until Rich Gordon leaked a copy

to the press, which earned him a sound scolding from the Sportsmen's president. Saving Admiralty, however, became a little more respectable.

Meanwhile, the Stellars thought it important that they affiliate with a national group, and so they became the Juneau Group of the Alaska Chapter of the Sierra Club. The Club's president, a San Francisco physician named Edgar Wayburn, visited southeast Alaska in 1967, the first official visit by an officer of the organization. Ed and his wife Peggy, who were subsequently to write numerous books and articles on Alaska, were greeted warmly by the Forest Service's regional forester, W. Howard Johnson, who threw a party in their honor.

Johnson formally greeted the Wayburns and then turned the floor over to the doctor. "Thank you, Mr. Johnson," said Dr. Wayburn. "We're most interested in your plans for this beautiful country. We're concerned, though—we didn't hear you say anything about wilderness."

"The whole God damn thing is wilderness, Ed," boomed back Johnson.

"Yes, but tomorrow or the next day it could be gone. The Sierra Club would like to see some wilderness protected legally and permanently," Dr. Wayburn replied.

Wayburn went on to suggest that the Forest Service could execute a master stroke. St. Regis had recently backed out of its agreement to log Admiralty Island, and Wayburn suggested that the agency make the entire island a wilderness area, a million-acre refuge for bear and eagle and deer.

Howard Johnson declined to react to Wayburn's suggestion, undoubtedly because his agency had already offered the island to U.S. Plywood. From the viewpoint of Cliff Lobaugh, Karl Lane, and the others, the future looked pretty bleak.

❧

In the summer of 1963 a law student from Harvard named Warren Matthews served as a clerk in the law offices of Lillick, McHose, Wheat, Adams & Charles in San Francisco. He worked under Don Harris, one of the Sierra Club's most active volunteer attorneys, on litigation involving maritime law: ship crashes and the like. Following graduation, Matthews moved to Anchorage and went to work for a large law firm, later setting up in a two-man practice, Matthews & Dunn. One day in 1969 he got a call from his old friend Don Harris.

The Sierra Club's got a problem down near Juneau, Harris told him, and wants to file a lawsuit. Are you interested?

"I was," Matthews said in a recent interview. "They had a lawsuit in mind but no legal theory to speak of. I was interested in the case and went ahead and put it together." (Matthews, at the time of this interview, was Chief Justice of the Alaska Supreme Court.)

Matthews's complaint argued that in making the Juneau Unit Sale the Forest Service would violate the Wilderness Act, the Multiple Use-Sustained Yield Act, the Endangered Species Act, and a series of Forest Service regulations that, in part, required the agency to sell timber at fair market value after

Starfish and urchins at low tide, Gambier Bay, Admiralty Island.

*Bald eagle (*Haliaeetus leucocephalus*) calling. By R. H. Armstrong/Animals Animals.*

*Black-tailed deer (*Odocoilus hemionus*). By Fletcher & Baylis/Photo Researchers, Inc.*

offering it at public auction. He filed suit on February 10, 1970, asking the court to invalidate the contract.

The heart of the suit was the multiple-use claim. Matthews's thesis was that the law required the Forest Service to manage its lands to benefit not only timber production but also recreation, watersheds, wildlife, and fish. Clearcutting an estimated 98.4 percent of the available commercial-grade timber was in no sense a multiple-use management plan, but rather a single-use plan that would eliminate or radically curtail the other possible uses.

Plaintiffs in the case were the Sierra Club, the Sitka Conservation Society, and Karl Lane, whose business stood to be severely damaged by the logging. Defendants were the Secretary of Agriculture, the Secretary of the Interior, and several of their subordinates. The state of Alaska intervened on behalf of the defense, though the state's Department of Fish and Game was not happy with the decision. U.S. Plywood, which by then had been acquired by Champion Paper Company, intervened as well. Plywood Champion stopped all preparation for logging and mill construction until the trial could be held and the dispute resolved.

Several other conservation groups tried to join the case on the side of the plaintiffs—the Alaska Conservation Society, the Tongass Conservation Society, the Alaska Mountaineering Club, the Southeast Mountaineering Club, and Friends of the Earth—but they were judged not to have standing.

The trial began on November 5, 1970. As is frequently the case, the government asserted a number of technical defenses. First, it challenged the standing of the plaintiffs, but club and society members were able to outline the frequent and historic uses they had made of Admiralty, and Karl Lane's

standing was clearly unimpeachable. Next the government invoked a legal doctrine called "laches," saying in effect that the plaintiffs had waited too long to bring suit, that Plywood–Champion had spent a substantial amount of money in good faith, and that it was too late to sue. The judge rejected the standing challenge and took the other under advisement.

By the time the trial was held, passions were high in Juneau. A motel marquee next to the road between the airport and town was emblazoned with "Sierra Club Go Home!" Fights broke out on school playgrounds between the sons of conservationists and the sons of would-be millworkers or loggers. People were tripped from behind in grocery stores. Someone tried to sink Karl Lane's boat. Warren Matthews was threatened as well, though he insists he didn't consider the threats serious. Throughout that period, as Cliff Lobaugh later remembered, "we got lots of criticism for aligning ourselves with a California outfit [the Sierra Club]. But when the lawsuit came along it was the other side that used all the outside talent."

The courtroom was packed. Judge Raymond Plummer called matters to order in this first conservation lawsuit in Alaska. Rich Gordon remembers, "There was Warren Matthews sitting on one side of the table and about twenty lawyers sitting on the other. Even though the Forest Service was the principal defendant, it was Manley Strayer, the lawyer for Plywood–Champion, who ran the show. The government lawyers didn't open their mouths unless Strayer told them to.

"Matthews was great, absolutely marvelous," said Gordon. "He did a terrific job of organizing the case. It gave a lot of us hope that we really might be able to stop this thing."

Matthews called a string of witnesses, among them a

number of employees of state natural resources agencies who had to take time off from work to testify. Ralph Young, the guide and writer, called the logging at Whitewater Bay and elsewhere "obscene," leaving behind a "wet desert." Charles Stoddard, a forester and former director of the Bureau of Land Management, testified that the Forest Service is biased in favor of timber production at the expense of other values. Dick Myron explained how cutting alongside salmon streams resulted not only in erosion and sedimentation but also in a rise in water temperature during the summer spawning season, which interferes with reproduction. Ed Wayburn testified to the Sierra Club's interest in the island (John Muir sailed around it and camped there in 1881, and the Sierra Club first suggested that the island be made a national park in 1932), and asserted that Admiralty was far more valuable to the nation as wilderness than as tree farm. Walter Mead, a forest economist from the University of California at Santa Barbara, reported that the price of wood had risen dramatically in the three years before the contract was signed with Plywood–Champion, and that the sale price was no longer anywhere near fair market value.

Matthews produced a map of eagle nests on the island put together by Fred Robards of the Fish and Wildlife Service. Cliff Lobaugh recalls that episode with a sparkle in his eye. "They plotted the nest sites on a blank sheet using just the coordinates. They came up with a bunch of dots on a piece of paper. Then they superimposed the paper on a map of Admiralty. It was an exact fit. There were blank places where logging had been carried out in the past; otherwise it was a perfect map of the island. Eagle nests are that close together. And the effects of logging were unmistakable."

As the trial progressed, a young biologist could sometimes be seen in the audience, keeping his ears open and his mouth closed. He was Reginald Barrett, from Berkeley, California. Armed with a brand-new Ph.D. in wildlife biology, he had undertaken a study of the probable effects of logging on the wildlife of Admiralty, under the direction of his mentor, A. Starker Leopold of the University of California at Berkeley. The study was financed by Plywood–Champion.

The whole arrangement was controversial, to put it mildly. In 1969, Karl R. Bendetsen, chairman of Plywood–Champion, had appointed a team of seven university ecologists, of whom Leopold was one, to advise the company on where to build its mill and how to log without damaging the multiple resources of the forest.

"Karl Bendetsen wanted to do it right," Barrett said later, "I really believe he did. But he was terribly naive about what's right. He thought he could sit a bunch of ecologists down in a room and they could tell him how he could have his cake and eat it too, how to log all those trees and not harm wildlife or watersheds."

Conservationists viewed this panel with grave apprehension, fearing that Plywood–Champion was simply buying itself some respectability, that the distinguished ecologists were being used by the company. But Starker Leopold insisted that they would do a fair and honest job, and that Bendetsen had promised to follow any recommendations that the panel might make. "Over and over, both in court and in front of the media, the lawyers and other spokesmen for Plywood–Champion repeated their promise that they would abide by the recommendations of their commission," Barrett says. "It was a great opportunity and a great responsibility. I can't tell you how many times they said, 'Reg Barrett is going to come up with the answers, and we'll do what he says.' It scared hell out of me." Bendetsen and Plywood–Champion would come to regret that promise, and to regret it deeply.

The first request to the panel of ecologists was to recommend a site for the new pulp and lumber mill. They selected Echo Cove at Berner's Bay on the mainland, about thirty miles north of Juneau. It would have been the largest structure of its kind in the world. "The mill site was the first order of business, and the easiest problem to solve," says Barrett. "But for the wildlife report, Starker decided he wanted some on-the-ground research."

Reg Barrett headed for Admiralty. First, he sailed around the island, into its bays, coves and inlets, with a team of fishery biologists from the University of Washington. They walked miles in the streams, noting the types and concentration of salmon, char, and trout. Five species of salmon spawn in Admiralty's streams, though each species has two names, so it can sound like more. (Chinook and king are the same, as are sockeye and red, silver and coho, pink and humpback, chum and dog.)

Scientists with the Alaska Department of Fish and Game had begun to notice problems with salmon reproduction in other areas that seemed to be caused by logging. "They were going bananas over this thing," says Barrett. "We were attempting to confirm what they were saying." Siltation from road-building and erosion following clearcuts was ruining spawning beds, and the removal of streamside trees was allowing water temperature to rise at critical times of the year, to the detriment of the fish, according to the Fish and Game scientists. Barrett and the fisheries group did find that the salmon runs in Whitewater Bay were much reduced, evidently as a result of the logging.

Next, Barrett began to catalog the terrestrial mammals, concentrating on brown bears and especially deer. Before he left for Alaska, Barrett had been counseled by Leopold to visit Urban Nelson, who before his retirement had served as the head of the U.S. Fish and Wildlife Service for Alaska. "He had figured out the deer problem with logging. He and Harry Merriam of the Alaska Department of Fish and Game deserve the credit for figuring out the deer problem," according to Barrett.

The problem, which Barrett documented in considerable detail over the next year, is this. The deer spend the summer and early fall in the higher-elevation meadows of the island, eating grasses, leaves, and berries and storing fat for the long

False hellebore, Admiralty Island.

cold winter. When snow begins to fall, they descend to the forest for shelter. As the snows fall harder and lie ever thicker on the ground, the deer retreat lower and lower on the mountains, spending the hardest part of the winter beneath the biggest trees near the water's edge. Only there, beneath the dense canopy of the climax forest, can they find shelter and a meager supply of food, a diet supplemented with seaweed they nibble on the beaches.

The trees the loggers most prize, for their size and their proximity to water and an easy ride to the mill, are the very trees the deer need to help them through the winter. Without the forest, reasoned Nelson, Merriam, and Barrett, the deer would be devastated, perhaps destroyed altogether. For life on Admiralty Island is no picnic. Every year, a large number of deer perish of natural causes over the winter. Some years — when the herd has grown large owing to a succession of mild winters and a hard winter follows — thousands of deer will starve, their carcasses frozen into snowbanks. They provide food for brown bears emerging from hibernation in spring, before the grasses and berries have appeared on the flats and the salmon have entered the streams. The deer had it rough enough as it was, thought these researchers. Taking away their most important defense against winter would almost certainly spell their demise.

Barrett made copious notes, took several thousand photographs, and repaired to Berkeley to write a report. It was early 1972.

In retrospect, he would say later, all the scientists and government and company officials were extremely helpful that year, with one notable exception. "I kept asking the company for its calculations of what volume of timber there was in the various stands on the island, and they kept telling me the data were in the Lower Forty-eight, or somewhere, in storage." This was a crucial piece of information, since what the company had bought was the right to log 8.75 billion board feet of timber, not a particular number of acres. If there was less commercial timber on the island than they thought, they'd have to cut every last tree to meet the contract. The Forest Service also refused to provide Barrett with its own surveys and estimates of timber volume on the island, a decision that was to embarrass the agency a few years later.

Meanwhile, the trial in Juneau ground to its conclusion. Warren Matthews had argued forcefully against the logging plan and its rationale: "The Forest Service is charged with the management of the national forests to provide an even flow of timber,

Mussels and seaweed, Gambier Bay, Admiralty Island.

range, water, recreation, wilderness. . . . It is not in their charge to work for the benefit of local economies," he said years later. "A pulp mill was proposed, also primary processing, all to benefit the local economy. If Congress had wanted the Forest Service to do economic planning it would have said so. It would have hired the agency some economists. The Forest Service was doing it [economic planning] anyway—and ruining the economy in the process by putting the mills in the wrong places. I think that was—and is—a good argument, a legally correct argument."

Matthews stressed also that the entire production of the mill would be exported to Japan, so the sacrifice of a million acres of forest would not even provide lumber and pulp to the American market. He argued that at the very least the Forest Service ought to be required to prepare an environmental impact statement on so large an action, characterized in the early stages of the litigation as "the single largest act of wilderness destruction ever contemplated."

Matthews made several other arguments, including one that would a few years later be accepted by a judge in West Virginia and lead to the wholesale rewriting of the laws the Forest Service operates under. Matthews had been reading an account of the creation of the Forest Service by its founder, Gifford Pinchot. In it, describing the conditions under which the agency would be permitted to sell trees from the public forests, Pinchot specified that trees for sale must be large, old, or mature and they must all be marked. That seemed pretty plainly to rule out clearcutting, where the marking is done on a map and everything is razed to the ground.

Judge Plummer retired to his chambers to mull over the arguments and evidence presented to him. He issued his ruling in five parts that stretched from March 25 to May 21, 1971. On every point he ruled against the plaintiffs, except on standing, though he went out of his way to point out that Karl Lane could easily find another island to take his customers to.

The plaintiffs' legal arguments were utterly without merit, he said, and what's more, they had waited too long to file their suit. He clearly felt that it was unseemly for these mere citizens to try to tell the Forest Service how to run its affairs. The Forest Service was the expert in these matters, the government agency charged by Congress with running the national forests. Its discretion would prevail. The opinion is as interesting for what it omits as for what it says. There is no mention of wildlife anywhere in twenty-six dense pages: no grizzlies, no eagles, no deer, no salmon found their way into Judge Plummer's opus. There is scarcely a mention of trees. To the judge, this was a dry legal matter; abstractions were more real than a living wilderness island.

Matthews promptly took an appeal to the Ninth Circuit Court of Appeals in San Francisco. He and Angus McBeth of the Natural Resources Defense Council argued the case in December 1971.

❧

After a year in the field, Reginald Barrett wrote a fifty-page report that came to a stern conclusion. As contemplated, the Plywood–Champion logging operation on Admiralty Island would devastate the island's wildlife: "Each major drainage that is totally cut wouldn't be able to support optimum wildlife populations for most of the next 100 years. . . . The days of massive clearcutting of whole watersheds have passed."

Barrett suggested two alternatives the company could adopt to mitigate the impact of the logging: reduce drastically the acreage to be logged, leaving corridors deer could use to reach the lowlands in winter and limiting the size of each cut, or stretch the logging out over a hundred years rather than fifty, effectively halving the amount of timber cut each year. Either course of action would involve renegotiating the contract between the company and the Forest Service, and Barrett suggested that Plywood–Champion might be able to persuade the agency to find timber off the island to substitute for what wasn't cut on Admiralty.

In November 1972, Starker Leopold approved the report and recommendations with minor editing and shipped it off to Bendetsen of Plywood–Champion. The original agreement between U.S. Plywood and Dr. Leopold provided that the company would have thirty days to comment on the report before it was made public. "A few days after the report was sent, Starker had lots of people in his office," Barrett remembers. "You could hear the commotion through the door. Five or six lawyers trying to persuade Starker to change the report. Starker wouldn't budge. I think he knew all along what was going to happen. Finally, they agreed that Bendetsen could include a letter with the report when it was released." The letter said in essence that the views expressed in the report were not necessarily those of the company.

A three-judge panel of the Ninth Circuit heard oral arguments on the appeal and let a year pass without announcing a decision. When Jim Moorman, who had just opened the Legal Defense Fund's first office and had joined the Admiralty defense team, received a copy of the Leopold-Barrett report, he immediately forwarded it to the court, with a request that Judge Plummer be ordered to hold a new trial to consider this new and devastating evidence. The court agreed, and sent the case back to Alaska. In the fall of 1974 Judge Plummer called to order a new trial.

In the meantime, Reg Barrett had taken a job with the Australian counterpart of the Fish and Wildlife service, studying feral pigs near Darwin. He flew to Anchorage to testify as the star witness for the plaintiffs. Most of his testimony concerned his report, and the likelihood that the logging would destroy a great deal of wildlife and habitat. The government's lawyers retorted that this was all old news. Similar studies had been reviewed by the Forest Service and given the "due consideration" required by law, the attorneys argued.

The night before, Moorman had burst into Barrett's hotel room with a sheaf of papers in his hand. "I think we've got some dynamite here," he said. The next day at the trial, Moorman produced the same documents. They were the Forest Service's calculations of how much timber there actually was within the boundaries of the Juneau Unit Sale—the information Barrett had sought for months in vain. "Have you ever seen these documents?" Moorman asked Barrett. He had not. "Did you ask to see them?" He had, repeatedly. The court was stunned, particularly the attorneys for the defense. The Forest Service was clearly going to have a difficult time arguing that it had made a sound decision when it refused to reveal the basis for the decision.

After the last witness testified, Judge Plummer recessed the trial, saying that he would ask for final arguments from both sides once he made up his mind what parts of the testimony he would accept as evidence and use to reach his decision. He never did. Nearly two years after the trial ended, with still no ruling from the judge, U.S. Plywood–Champion bailed out. The Japanese buyer of the lumber and pulp, Kanzaki Paper Manufacturing Company, had pulled out of its end of the agreement, citing changed economic circumstances, and Plywood–Champion had had enough. In 1976 it forfeited its $100,000 deposit and told the Forest Service it was no longer interested in the deal. Admiralty's forests were spared, at least for a time, and defenders of the island pressed their campaign to have it preserved permanently.

❧

On December 18, 1971, Congress passed the Alaska Native Claims Settlement Act. The act awarded a total of 44 million unspecified acres of land and a billion dollars to people who could prove that they were at least one-fourth Alaskan Indian, Eskimo, Aleut, or a combination thereof (which set off a considerable search for birth certificates, oral histories, and the like).

To get all this organized, the act created a series of native corporations, with natives born on or before December 18, 1971, as shareholders. Each village had its own corporation, as did cities. Over these were imposed thirteen regional corporations to coordinate the local corporations and create region-wide cultural and economic enterprises.

Each corporation was given the right to select several tens of thousands of acres, depending on the population of the village or city and its location. The corporations were generally expected to take the lands surrounding their villages and towns. Regional corporations were given doughnuts of land surrounding the selections of the lesser corporations in their regions. All were given a daunting order, to go along with this top-down imposition of capitalism on an unprepared society: start making money. This requirement to make money has

Devil's club in fall color, near Angoon, Admiralty Island.

driven the native corporations to accelerate the exploitation of natural resources to the point where that exploitation is simply not sustainable, and many have had severe economic difficulties. As an Eskimo testified at an Interior Department hearing, "They set us down and said, 'You're a corporation, now act like one.' It would be like setting a bunch of Wall Street people down in the Arctic and saying, 'Now go catch a whale.' "

This laying-on of corporations has also, in some instances, pitted one group of natives against another, a tragic and unintended side effect of the laudable effort to cut Alaskan natives in for a fair share of the land's wealth. Perhaps the most acrimonious such situation is on Admiralty Island.

In 1976, as soon as the timber sale collapsed, three native corporations announced their intention of selecting lands on Admiralty. Kootznoowoo, the corporation for Angoon, claimed land surrounding the village. Goldbelt, representing the natives of Juneau, and Shee Atika, representing the natives of Sitka, selected land north and south of Angoon, in some of Angoon's prime hunting and fishing grounds. Goldbelt picked a mitten-shaped parcel on the northwest coast of the island. The fingers reached up into three watersheds, two with lakes in them. The heel of the hand touched the coast at a spot called Cube Cove. Shee Atika carved its township from lands surrounding Hood and Chaik bays on the southwest coast, areas that Karl Lane had argued were the most important to protect.

Round two of the battle for Admiralty had begun. It didn't take long for the action to move back to court. When Shee Atika and Goldbelt announced their selections, Cecil Andrus, President Jimmy Carter's Secretary of the Interior, tried to reduce the size of the parcels and persuade the two corporations to take land elsewhere. Shee Atika and Goldbelt responded by filing suit against the government. The Sierra Club Legal Defense Fund intervened on the side of the defense, represented by Joe Brecher, a lawyer who had a great deal of experience in litigation involving native Americans through his work with the Native American Rights Fund.

As this litigation was being played out, Secretary Andrus and President Carter took an aggressive step. Back in 1972, the native claims act had set aside 80 million acres of Alaska's most beautiful places and ordered the Interior Department to recommend to Congress which of these lands should be preserved as parks, refuges, and the like. Those withdrawals were to last for five years, ample time for Congress to confirm, reject, or modify the recommendations. Five years later, despite several attempts, Congress still had not approved legislation to create parks, refuges, or wild rivers on those lands. As of December 17, 1978, those 80 million acres would be available to the state to do with as it pleased.

It was an open secret, however, that President Carter and Secretary Andrus had been investigating ways they might act to preserve the lands should Congress fail to. Indeed, indications were so strong that the state of Alaska filed a preëmptive suit in November 1978, asking the court to be on the lookout for a land grab by the administration.

On December 1, using discretionary powers granted them

under a variety of laws—primarily the Antiquities Act of 1906 and the Federal Land Planning and Management Act of 1976—Andrus and Carter moved to set aside nearly 100 million acres of Alaskan wildlands to give Congress extra time to enact appropriate legislation. Admiralty Island was declared a national monument, with logging forbidden. Spared again—but the battle was far from over.

Next, the state of Alaska sued Carter, claiming that the president had locked up lands the state ought to be able to select for itself under the Statehood Act of 1958. Stephan Volker, who had opened an office for the Legal Defense Fund in Juneau at the beginning of 1978, joined the case on the side of the President. "I'm not sure most Americans realize how important that withdrawal by Jimmy Carter was," Volker recalls. "It took some courage to take that step. Carter was deeply committed to the preservation of Alaska; the country owes him a great deal for what he did."

Kootznoowoo and Goldbelt meanwhile had agreed to trade their claims on Admiralty for lands elsewhere, with two exceptions: Angoon kept land immediately adjacent to the village, and, before the off-island switch was made, Goldbelt swapped its holdings for those of Shee Atika. Thus, the places most highly prized by Karl Lane—Hood and Chaik bays—were added safely to the monument. Only the Cube Cove selection remained under threat of logging.

And that last problem was nearly resolved by the Alaska National Interest Lands Conservation Act of 1980. That law was the culmination of what many consider the conservation movement's finest campaign. It took many years, thousands upon thousands of hours of work by people in just about every community in every state, from every environmental organization and association. It confirmed and improved upon the bold Andrus/Carter stroke of 1978, setting aside more than 100 million acres of Alaska's most beautiful lands in national parks, national monuments, wild and scenic rivers, wildlife refuges, and several other categories of reservation.

Admiralty's status as a national monument—managed by the U.S. Forest Service rather than the Park Service, a vestige of its origins in the Tongass National Forest—was preserved. So, unfortunately, was the inholding. A last-minute maneuver by Senator Ted Stevens authorized the conveyance of the Cube Cove township to Shee Atika.

The statute itself had two contradictory provisions. It said that all of Admiralty Island except for the Mansfield Peninsula on the far northern tip of the island—the land nearest Juneau—was in the national monument and was off limits to logging. It also said, however, that Shee Atika had the right to claim its 23,040 acres near Cube Cove and, by implication, to sell the trees if it chose to do so. It was quite clear from the debate that preceded passage of the bill that the key congressional players hoped and expected Shee Atika to trade its Cube Cove holdings for land off the island, but that was not explicitly required by the legislation.

Enter James Watt, Ronald Reagan's first Secretary of the Interior. His antipathy for environmental organizations was

Village of Angoon, west coast of Admiralty Island.

evident well before he took his new job, and he wasted little time when the Admiralty matter came before him. In December 1981 he conveyed the Cube Cove township to Shee Atika.

Shee Atika made immediate preparations to begin logging, and the Legal Defense Fund headed back to the courthouse, this time led by Durwood Zaelke, an attorney who had worked in the Carter Justice Department under Jim Moorman, after Moorman left the Legal Defense Fund. This litigation, and the myriad cases that followed, were pursued jointly by the environmentalists and the residents of Angoon, the tiny village on the west coast of the island that had been decimated by the United States military a century before and was now fighting to protect its fishing and hunting lands.

For Angoon, the battle was for survival, not only of the deer and fish and other resources they depended on for food and shelter, but also of their culture and traditions. More than any other village, Angoon had maintained the Tlingit tradition. Angoon is to the Tlingit what Oraibi is to the Hopi. Other Tlingit villages had adopted western ways, given up the old ceremonies such as the potlatch, and ceased passing the tribal stories from old to young. Angoon was by no means primitive — it had electricity, a few telephones, an automobile or two, a government school, a general store — but it remained close to the old ways and fiercely determined to stay that way.

"I don't know how many environmental impact studies they've done over the years," said Ed Gambell, mayor of Angoon in 1988, "but they never take us into account. Our elders have a saying. Admiralty Island is a bowl. You're welcome to drink, but don't chip the bowl. If you damage this bowl, you don't know if you've chipped the rim or put a hole through the bottom."

Starting with the suit against Watt, lawsuits and appeals flew like sawdust from a chainsaw with little let-up for a half-dozen years. Zaelke represented the Sierra Club and The Wilderness Society. The firm of Furth, Fahrner & Bloemle in San Francisco represented Angoon. The Anchorage firm of Bailey and Mason assisted both plaintiffs, who accused Watt of flouting the Alaska National Interest Lands Act by trying to give away part of a national monument to a group that admittedly planned to log it.

The Corps of Engineers gave its permission to Shee Atika for a log-transfer facility at Cube Cove, so Zaelke sued the Corps. Then, to evade Corps jurisdiction, Shee Atika said it would airlift logs by helicopter out into Chatham Strait and drop them into state waters. The Legal Defense Fund sued the state.

At one stage, thinking all was settled, Shee Atika invited the mayor of Angoon to attend a tree-cutting ceremony at Cube

Cove. Instead the mayor phoned Zaelke, who rushed to court and got a last-minute restraining order forbidding the cutting. The Legal Defense Fund also filed a *lis pendens,* a legal notice that warns the world that ownership of a certain piece of property is the subject of a legal battle. Shee Atika thereupon sued the Sierra Club for damaging its ability to borrow money by filing the *lis pendens.* Angoon sued the government for failing to protect its subsistence hunting and fishing grounds.

Matters reached a point where the Legal Defense Fund reported that it had persuaded the court to issue eight injunctions and restraining orders in a period of eighteen months. All this time negotiations were proceeding to find land elsewhere that Shee Atika could trade for its Admiralty holdings. At one point Congress came close to imposing a land exchange, but last minute pressure from the timber industry scuttled the bill in the Senate after it had passed the House.

In the fall of 1986 the Ninth Circuit Court of Appeals finally washed its hands of the case, saying, "This litigation is the latest episode in a twelve-year struggle which reflects badly upon the ability of the three branches of the federal government to resolve disputes reasonably expeditiously." The last legal remedy had been exhausted. When the Supreme Court declined to review the decision, the case was closed.

Buck Parker, the Legal Defense Fund's coordinating attorney, has hiked extensively on Admiralty. He summed up the experience this way: "The legal battles over Admiralty Island left all but 23,040 acres of a million-acre national monument wild, which amounts to more than ninety-seven percent. That's not bad. And, as of late 1989, one of the three Cube Cove watersheds remains uncut, 8,000 acres of the 23,000-acre inholding. Efforts continue to preserve it via purchase or exchange. Admiralty remains a reasonably impregnable bear fortress, a redoubt for eagles and black-tailed deer. We're proud of what we helped accomplish, and happy to have been of service to the Tlingit of the island."

And what of Angoon, as it comes to terms with the late twentieth century? A glance at the provisions offered at the one general store gives a bit of the flavor of the place. At Angoon Trading one can purchase fan belts, hibachis, oarlocks, stationery, clothes (most everybody in Angoon seems to wear sweatshirts that say "Admiralty National Monument—Keep it Wild"), fishing gear, day-old papers, *Playboy,* batteries, nonprescription drugs, propane stoves, Duraflame logs(!), jacks, axes, heaters, television sets, games, flashlights, hardwood dowels (imported from Nashville, Tennessee), carpenter's tools, plumbing supplies, kids' toys, coffee cups, pet food, electrical equipment, and sundry groceries. No beer, wine, or liquor. In fact, on July 26, 1988, the residents of Angoon voted to outlaw even possession of alcoholic beverages for personal consumption (sale was already illegal), a self-imposed prohibition it is hoped will curb the alcoholism that plagues native settlements in Alaska. Down the way from Angoon Trading, a small enterprise is underway where Angoon residents assemble computer components made in Asia and sell them to agencies of the state of Alaska. Also very much in evidence are the smokehouses for salmon and the boats residents use to fish and travel to deer-hunting grounds.

Ed Gambell, the mayor, runs Angoon from a second-floor office in a spiffy new building on a hill above town. He's grateful to the lawyers who have helped preserve his island. He smiles at his visitor. "We'll make it," he says. "We're natives. We have all the patience in the world."

Islands in Gambier Bay, Admiralty Island National Monument.

CHAPTER THREE

Around the Colorado Plateau
The Politics of Energy

The Colorado Plateau is a land of wild colors and bizarre shapes, of searing heat and icy cold, of sand and scorpions and vistas so dramatic they can leave you breathless. The Colorado River and hundreds of tributaries carved this land, aided by wind and rain and snow and ice. They gouged into the ground as the ground slowly rose to greet them, cutting through layer after layer of sandstone and mud and shale and coal. Left behind were arches and bridges and rincons and goosenecks and cottonwood-lined streams and pink-streaked cliffs.

A glance at the river's handiwork in the latter part of the twentieth century (it hasn't finished the job) shows roughly 15,000 square miles of the driest, wildest, gaudiest, least populated, part of the American landscape. All those adjectives made the plateau a shrine for conservationists (and for many Native Americans as well, as we shall see), and led to the creation of a half-dozen national parks, a brace of national recreation areas, a score of national monuments, a hat trick of national forests, several state parks, and many reserves set aside to preserve prehistoric ruins. Most of the rest remains in federal ownership, under the indifferent jurisdiction of the Bureau of Land Management. It is a land much admired but until recently little visited. It is not, of course, completely unknown.

Sandstone formation, a few miles west of proposed coal-fired power-plants on Salt Wash, Capitol Reef National Park, Utah.

*Sunrise, the Virgin River, southern Utah. Conservationists are currently engaged in a
battle with development interests over rights to the river's water.*

First colonizers were the mysterious Anasazi Indians, who
built an elaborate civilization and then vanished. They were
followed by the Hopi, the Navajo, and many more tribes. John
Wesley Powell made the first descent of the Colorado River in
1869. Soon came the Mormons, followed by other white settlers. They farmed, raised livestock, built towns and cities.
Tourists and wilderness fanciers came too, and the inevitable
disagreements about the uses of wild land began.

The first major resource arguments concerned water and
schemes to use it for irrigation and generating electricity. The
biggest fights—over dams in Grand Canyon and Dinosaur National Monument—are chronicled well elsewhere and did not
involve litigation in a major way, so they will be passed over
in this book. Current water struggles that occupy conservationists and their lawyers include not only hydroelectric and
irrigation projects, but also the thorny subject of water
rights, which is being fought out in several courthouses and
legislatures.

There is a map dated 1975 pinned to the wall in my office, yel-
lowed, hand-drawn, deeply creased. It depicts all the powerplants, stripmines, and powerlines expected to be built on the

Colorado Plateau between that date and approximately 1990.
It is almost impossible to comprehend the scale of environmental degradation that would have occurred if all those
projects had been completed.

Several attractive features drew the attention of power companies, government energy planners, and others to that spectacular part of the country at that time. One was coal, lots
of coal, all over the place, most of it far lower in sulfur than
Appalachian coal—sulfur having been identified as a substance
injurious to human lungs. It is also bad for forests, lakes,
streams, and crops, as we learned in the 1980s with the growing
scourge of acid rain.

A second attraction of western coal, from an economic
point of view, is that much of it lies near the surface, which
means that it can be stripmined. This is a great deal less expensive than deep mining, unless environmental factors are included in the calculations. If the full costs of reclaiming
stripmined sites are figured in—assuming reclamation is possible at all—then deep mining sometimes looks more attractive. Nonetheless, in the mid-1960s the low-sulfur, shallow
coalfields of the Southwest looked like a bonanza waiting to
be reaped.

This was a time when energy consumption was growing
at astronomical rates: six, seven, even eight percent per year.

Water-pocked sandstone, Island in the Sky, Canyonlands National Park, Utah.

The Five Faces petroglyph, Davis Canyon, Canyonlands National Park.

Simple arithmetic should have shown planners that such a growth rate could not be sustained for long—seven percent annual growth means that consumption would double in ten years and double again after another ten. Before long we would be consuming more investment capital—not to mention water, steel, and other commodities—than was available for all uses, including schools, factories, and the nation's defense. Nonetheless, it was assumed that energy consumption would continue to grow at this rate for decades.

To the planners there were other major pluses for the Southwest as well. First, the air was as clear as air can be; it was where asthmatics and tuberculosis patients were sent to get away from smoke and dust. Indeed, a government survey of air contaminants on the plateau in the 1960s could find none. Not one part per million or one part per billion; none. It was said that an Indian on a high bluff in the Navajo Nation could see the dust from a single horseback rider at a distance of thirty miles.

What made this attractive to energy planners was that the air in and around cities in the East, Midwest, and West was by then seriously sullied. Laws and regulations were being implemented that were making it all but impossible to construct new coal-burning powerplants anywhere near cities. One solution was to build new plants out in the country.

A serious drawback of western coal was that most of it is not very rich in energy. But this too supported the wisdom of building powerplants in the wide-open spaces. To compensate for the inefficiency of the western coal and the cost of transporting millions of tons to distant plants to be burned, a new concept was devised: the mine-mouth powerplant. This would solve many problems at once. The coal would not have to be delivered hundreds or thousands of miles by rail, and the smoke from burning the coal would not pollute the lungs of city dwellers. Instead, the electricity would be produced on-site at the mine and sent off to voracious energy consumers in Los Angeles, Las Vegas, Tucson, Phoenix, and anywhere else willing to pay for it. Recent advances in the technology of electricity transmission seemed to make the idea feasible.

The promoters of massive industrialization in the Southwest didn't bank on several other factors, however. The area may have been sparsely populated, but it was not entirely without human inhabitants. There were, for example, some twenty-four Indian reservations, by far the largest of which is the Navajo Reservation, a sprawling empire bigger than a half-dozen eastern states. The Navajo, the Hopi, the Apache, the Zuni, and a score of other Native American tribes had lived relatively peacefully in those lands for thousands of years. The Indians, like indigenous people in most of the world, had little real power in their dealings with white men, but they would put up more resistance than anyone expected.

In addition to the natives, there were a great many other Americans who loved the area just the way it was and were appalled at the thought of turning it into another Gary, Indiana.

The proposals on various drawing boards—the icons on my aging map—added up to the following:

NAME	NUMBER OF UNITS	CAPACITY (IN MEGAWATTS)	SCHEDULE
Four Corners	5	2,085	1963–70
Mojave	2	1,510	1971
San Juan	3	990	1973–80
Navajo	3	2,310	1974–76
Huntington Canyon	1	430	1974
Kaiparowits	6	5,000	1978–89
Intermountain	6	3,000	1980–85
Harry Allen	4	2,500	1985–90
Warner Valley	2	500	1985–87
Totals	*32*	*18,325*	

This would have been a huge concentration of powerplants in one area, a clustering that led some to suggest the phrase "national sacrifice area" for places whose natural resources would be sacrificed for the convenience of people far away. See the map in the front of this book for an idea of how dense the cluster would have been.

The government was in the process of preparing environmental impact analyses for each plant, but it refused to conduct a study of the entire project, saying it was just a coincidence that all these plants happened to be grouped the way they were. Such a study would reveal just what a catastrophe this mammoth development scheme would be.

At this stage the litigation was carried on mainly on behalf of several Indian tribes and handled by the Native American Rights Fund, one of whose lawyers, Joe Brecher, would later prosecute scores of cases for the Legal Defense Fund. They sued to demand a comprehensive environmental study of all the powerplants together. They sued to stop the stripmining of Black Mesa, a site sacred to the Hopi. They sued to bring the powerplants under the jurisdiction of the Federal Power Commission as a way to get some political leverage over matters. Some cases were initially successful, others were not. They did generate considerable public interest in the Colorado Plateau and the skirmishes being fought out there.

The most successful approach, for a time, was tried by Tony Ruckel, who had just opened the Legal Defense Fund's first branch office, in Denver. His idea was to bring a suit under the common-law theory of nuisance, and his suggested target was the air pollution being emitted by the Four Corners plant, the first two units of which had been sullying the landscape since 1963.

The Four Corners plant is situated in New Mexico and owned by four public utilities of which the biggest is Public Service of Arizona. Ruckel and the New Mexico Attorney General filed suit in state court against the operators of the plant seeking to abate the nuisance caused by its operation.

The trial court judge, Frank Zinn, agreed to hear the case, but the defendants claimed that a new state air pollution control agency was responsible for regulating plants such as Four Corners and that therefore the case should be dismissed. Zinn stood firm, but the New Mexico Supreme Court eventually sided with the utilities and tossed the plaintiffs out of court. Another rebuff.

But these lawyers were persistent. As many of them will say twenty years later, they were creating law. There was little to work with, and if one tactic failed they'd simply try another. With a combination of inventive thinking, hard work, and a dash of good luck, they could frequently find a solution to almost any problem.

The lawyers decided that if they couldn't block construction of the plants they should at least ensure that they be as clean-burning as possible. "Scrubbers," devices that remove up to ninety-five percent of sulfur from stack gases, had been invented by then, and Joe Brecher petitioned the Environmental Protection Agency to require scrubbers on all new plants, under regulations setting "New Source Performance Standards" or NSPS. (The air pollution bureaucracy and literature are as replete with acronyms and initials as anything in officialdom, maybe repleter.) The EPA refused. Brecher sued. The court said that a lawsuit was premature but that the EPA had better reconsider the request and take it seriously.

The EPA and the utilities had pretended to solve the problem of powerplant pollution simply by building enormously tall stacks—nearly 800 feet tall in some cases—in the vain hope that winds would disappear the problem. In the East this technique simply vaulted Ohio River pollution over the border to the Northeast and Canada. In the Southwest it introduced the Rocky Mountains to acid rain.

The EPA went along with the ruse by permitting the utility companies to measure pollution concentrations at ground level at the powerplants. With 775-foot stacks looming overhead, it was easy to stay under the pollution limits. Higher up was another story. A monitor that was eventually placed atop Shiprock, a 7,178-foot-high volcanic plug that soars above the desert near the Four Corners, found pollution concentrations that would have been illegal at ground level.

In the 1977 amendments to the Clean Air Act, Congress told the EPA to stop this sham. Nonetheless the EPA failed to issue the required regulations by the time Congress told it to. Howard Fox of the Legal Defense Fund filed suit, asking the court to force the EPA to obey the law. The court eventually did just that, and the tall-stacks gambit is a thing of the past.

Meanwhile, the EPA had been typically tardy in issuing its promised rules on scrubbers, so Joe Brecher again petitioned the agency. After a lengthy administrative proceeding, the agency agreed to require scrubbers on all new coal-fired electric powerplants. This was a major improvement in the status quo, but not perfect. The EPA required removal of only seventy percent of the stack-gas sulfur even though western utilities were stating publicly that removal of more than ninety percent was technically possible and economically feasible.

Back in the early 1970s, yet another tack was explored. A new Clean Air Act had passed Congress in 1970, and the fledgling Environmental Protection Agency was putting together regulations that would carry out the purposes of that

Act. An announcement was expected by summer 1971.

On April 30, 1971, the EPA released draft regulations that, among other things, explicitly forbade the "significant deterioration" of air quality in regions where air was still clean. "Prevention of significant deterioration," known as PSD, had first appeared in regulations issued by the National Air Pollution Control Agency in 1969. PSD was a key to keeping the West from becoming a dumping ground for big-city pollution.

Then, on August 14, the EPA issued its final regulations, and PSD had disappeared. In its place was a paragraph saying quite frankly that clean-air areas could indeed be legally polluted, just so long as they didn't get dirtier than a certain standard. The sacrifice of the West's air was official policy.

Bruce Terris filed suit for the Legal Defense Fund. Terris had been a classmate of Don Harris in law school, and he handled many Legal Defense Fund cases in the organization's first half-decade. He hung his suit on three words in the Clean Air Act, words that committed the country to an effort to "protect and enhance" air quality. "How can you 'enhance' air quality," Terris asked, "if you're allowing significant deterioration of that same air quality?" The EPA retorted that if Congress had wanted PSD regulations it should have said so, in so many words.

This time the conservationists struck gold, and the result goes to show that it doesn't take a long and complicated opinion to accomplish something significant. Judge John Pratt of the District Court for the District of Columbia took only four pages to find that yes, Congress must have meant to require prevention of significant deterioration when it wrote "protect and enhance." He blocked implementation of the EPA's regulations.

The government took an appeal, and the Court of Appeals sustained Judge Pratt without writing an opinion of its own. Next the case went to the Supreme Court, which agreed to review it and then deadlocked four to four; in that rare circumstance the judgment of the lower court is affirmed and no opinion is issued. So one of the most important legal principles in the control of air pollution in America was established by an almost perfunctory district court opinion and sustained by two higher courts with no further words being written. Brevity has its virtues. Eventually the principle of PSD was written explicitly into the Clean Air Act via amendments adopted by Congress in 1977.

The wrangling over PSD stretched out over several years, however, and the plans for bigger and bigger powerplants were steaming ahead. Indeed, litigation over PSD regulations continued right through the 1980s as the government repeatedly balked at issuing regulations to control various air pollutants. In fact, it was necessary as recently as 1986 for Legal Defense Fund attorney Deborah Reames to sue the Environmental Protection Agency to force issuance of long-delayed regulations to control industrial emissions of oxides of nitrogen.

Meanwhile, the Four Corners, Mojave, and Navajo powerplants were already operating or getting ready to. The next brick in the wall was to be Kaiparowits, a gigantic facility on a wild and remote plateau just south of the Escalante River

Cottonwoods in Harris Wash, a side canyon of the Escalante River, at the foot of the Kaiparowits Plateau.

Juniper and pinyon on Murphys Point, Canyonlands National Park.

and north of the Paria River, west of Lake Powell. Kaiparowits was expected eventually to comprise a half-dozen units with a capacity of 5,000 megawatts, fueled with coal from an underground mine nearby. It would pump 300 tons of ash, sulfur, and other contaminants into the air each *day*. (The Four Corners plant, at just over 2,000 megawatts less than half the size of Kaiparowits, already emitted more fly ash and soot than the cities of New York and Los Angeles combined.) The Kaiparowits plant would, if constructed, generate as much electricity as five of the biggest nuclear powerplants and ship the power to Los Angeles and San Diego.

As activists demonstrated and counter-demonstrated (some worthies in the town of Kanab, Utah, burned Robert Redford in effigy for opposing the powerplant), Tony Ruckel made his way to Los Angeles looking for help. He paid a call on a new public-interest law firm called the Center for Law in the Public Interest. The Center had been started by four young lawyers from the Los Angeles firm O'Melveny & Myers, including Fredric Sutherland. A Southern California native, Rick Sutherland attended San Diego State College and UCLA Law School. In 1977, Sutherland would move to San Francisco and take over as Executive Director of the Sierra Club Legal Defense Fund.

Ruckel sat down with the lawyers from the Center and said: we need help. Southern California Edison and San Diego Gas and Electric are about to ruin southern Utah in order to light the lights in southern California. Can't something be done on this end?

Rick Sutherland thought it could. "We'd been doing some public utilities work and we thought there must be a way to make California law apply. The utilities ought to have to get a certificate of public convenience and necessity—and get it before they started spending big money," he recalled years later.

In California, public utilities—privately owned monopolies—are regulated by the Public Utilities Commission, which is appointed by the governor. The commission sets rates, considers ratepayer complaints, and generally tries to keep the utilities in line. A certificate of public convenience and necessity is the commission's assurance that a project is needed and that the ratepayers won't get overcharged for the facility and the service it provides. Applying for such a certificate is an extensive, expensive process. Once the certificate is issued it all but guarantees that the commission will allow the utility to pass its costs along to its customers.

"Whether a certificate was required for out-of-state projects was an unresolved legal question at the time," Sutherland said. "What's more, if we could get the PUC to require the utilities to apply for a certificate, it would be tantamount to an

Junction Butte and sandstone formations, Monument Basin, Canyonlands National Park.

injunction against the project." Sutherland and his colleague, Brent Rushforth, filed a petition with the PUC asking that it require an application for a certificate. Briefs were passed back and forth. The hearings droned on for some weeks. Then came the day for final arguments, after which the hearing officer would make a recommendation to the full Public Utilities Commission. "Right at the outset a man from Southern California Edison stood up and read a prepared statement, a press release, to the court," Sutherland recalls. "It was complete capitulation. Both utilities were pulling out. The project was being cancelled.

"The hearing officer called a recess. We went out in the hall and went crazy." As John Hoffman, who preceded Sutherland as executive director of the Legal Defense Fund wrote later, "Kaiparowits had waived extradition and surrendered."

Edison and SDG&E then moved to have the proceeding dismissed as moot. The plant was cancelled, they argued, so there's no need for the Commission to rule on whether a certificate of public convenience and necessity is needed. The utilities, quite clearly, didn't want to be saddled with the certification requirement in future interstate projects.

Sutherland and Rushforth pressed ahead, however, wanting to nail down this important procedural point, and won a ruling from the commission that plants outside the boundaries of the state are subject to the certification procedure just as in-state plants are.

The clean-air champions were not allowed to rest on their laurels. In 1976 the Los Angeles Department of Water and Power, together with some Utah towns, announced their intention to build a gigantic complex of plants at Salt Wash, just to the east of Capitol Reef National Park. It was to be called the Intermountain Power Project. IPP was immediately dubbed "son of Kaiparowits," and the battle resumed. Only this time, the PUC gambit was not available—as a city-owned utility, LADWP was not under the jurisdiction of the commission.

Tony Ruckel, leaning heavily on the victory won by Bruce Terris in the PSD case, sent a formal petition to the new Secretary of the Interior, Cecil Andrus. He pointed out that IPP would sit between Capitol Reef and Canyonlands National Parks, not far from Glen Canyon National Recreation Area. Andrus found the argument persuasive. He halved the size of the plant and moved it a hundred miles north and west, well away from the canyon country.

Still, the California public utilities hankered for Utah's clean air. Next came a proposal from San Diego Gas & Electric, Southern California Edison, the Sacramento Municipal Utilities District, and Pacific Gas & Electric for a pair of power-plants. One, a 500-megawatt facility, would be built in and known as Warner Valley, near Hurricane, Utah, eighteen short miles from Zion National Park. The second, named Harry Allen for the Chairman of Nevada Power and Light, would be near Las Vegas, on the border of the Desert National Wildlife Refuge. It would have a capacity of 2,500 megawatts. Both would require the blessing of the Public Utilities Commission.

As if the plants weren't troublesome enough, the coal to feed them was to be stripped from deposits in the Alton Hills, located just outside, and in full view, of the Yovimpa Point overlook in Bryce Canyon National Park. That view was described by one T. C. Bailey in 1876 as "the wildest and most beautiful scene that the eye of man ever beheld." How much better it would be with draglines, dust, and, for good measure, the rumble and grind of heavy machinery.

The Surface Mining Control and Reclamation Act, a long-sought piece of legislation that President Ford had vetoed, finally became law during the Carter administration. While it was far weaker than conservationists had hoped, it did contain a novel provision: the Interior Secretary was empowered to declare certain areas "unsuitable" for stripmining. The Alton Hills seemed to fit that description.

Legal Defense Fund staff attorney Bill Curtiss drafted the first such petition to be filed with Secretary Andrus. Curtiss asked that the secretary declare the entire 325,000-acre coalfield at Alton unsuitable for stripmining because of its proximity to Bryce Canyon. There followed a string of public hearings at which, in a startling departure from precedent, a group of Mormon ranchers voiced their opposition to the project, mainly because of all the water it would consume. Then came a vigorous set of adversary proceedings before three federal agencies, one state agency, and the federal district court in Utah. Eventually Secretary Andrus declared the 210,000 acres closest to Bryce Canyon off limits to stripmining.

This was December 1980, as the Carter people were clearing out their desks, awaiting the arrival of the new Reagan administration and its environmental wrecking crew led by the unlikely James Watt. The utilities hoping to build the Allen/Warner Valley system sued Andrus, claiming that he had acted illegally in putting Alton off limits. The Legal Defense Fund intervened in that case to make sure that the new Interior Department defended itself vigorously and, for good measure, filed suit itself to have the 115,000 acres left out by Andrus also declared unsuitable.

Then Watt arrived and took command. It was clear that he would try to remake the agencies and their policies to suit his outlook, which was contrary to conservation philosophy in almost every conceivable respect. He seemed to favor exploring for oil wherever a geologist suggested there might be a drop. He boosted coal mining as a way to throw off the shackles of the Middle East. He derided the entire conservation movement as "environmental extremists."

To the surprise of no one, Watt decided to "reconsider" Andrus's unsuitability declaration. There followed a long, complicated, but ultimately inconclusive legal battle, with the coal companies claiming the unsuitability declaration was illegal and the Legal Defense Fund insisting that Watt's reconsideration was illegal.

Meanwhile, in California, Bill Curtiss had been keeping a close watch on the Public Utilities Commission and another, newer state regulatory body known as the California Energy Commission. The Energy Commission had some responsibilities in the approval of energy projects, and specifically in the

Winter at Bryce Canyon National Park, Utah.

Cottonwood trunks, Lavender Canyon, near the site of the proposed nuclear waste dump.

approval of powerline corridors. Briefs were written, hearings were held, and, in a near carbon copy of the Kaiparowits drama, the California sponsors of the project dropped out six days before final briefs were due to be filed. Another set of plants disappeared, although Curtiss would have preferred to fight to the finish and win a ringing vote from the commission. "We never got the shootout we wanted," he said later. "Someone always left town."

The shootout may yet happen. As of late 1988 there was a new proposal for a powerplant near Las Vegas. There are rumblings of new attempts to mine the coal near Bryce that is still "suitable," and a plan for a big new plant on the Navajo Reservation in the San Juan River basin. The campaign to keep the Southwest's air from looking more and more like Los Angeles' will perforce continue.

Coal—the mining, burning, and slurrying of it, the transmission of its electricity—has sparked the greatest environmental struggles on the Colorado Plateau in recent years. But there have been many others, several of which concern the energy-supply system once trumpeted by conservationists as the salvation for rivers threatened by hydroelectric dams. We speak of nuclear power, the mighty atom.

The existence of uranium under the Colorado Plateau has been known for many years. A brochure handed to visitors at Capitol Reef National Park contains a map that shows, in an obscure part of the park, a uranium mine that closed in the early 1900s. The uranium ore taken from these mines was used for watch dials and in medications. Not until scientists working on the atomic bomb produced a controlled chain reaction did anyone seriously suggest nuclear fission as a technique for producing electricity. When they did, however, there was a uranium rush in the West, with modern-day sourdoughs trading in their gold pans for geiger counters and bumping over the washes and mesas of Utah and Nevada in search of wealth.

They found a considerable amount of uranium, but the uncertain progress of the nuclear experiment has kept demand in check. Nonetheless, many attempts have been made to open uranium mines in the Plateau region, and this in turn has brought about a considerable amount of litigation for the Legal Defense Fund. Cases have involved lands near Grand Canyon, in Glen Canyon National Recreation Area, in Lake Mead National Recreation Area, and elsewhere. To date, most uranium mining has been blocked at the most sensitive areas.

The mining of uranium is generally referred to as the first step in the nuclear fuel cycle, which is something of a misnomer

Sky reflecting off wet sandstone, Zion National Park, Utah.

Evening light on grass and sandstone fins, Arches National Park, Utah.

since this cycle never repeats itself, never closes a loop. But then, the nuclear enterprise boasts one of the grandest collections of misnomers yet invented by the imagination of man, so one oughtn't be surprised. The end of the cycle is the disposal of used-up nuclear materials, "disposal" being another misnomer. Since some of the materials remain dangerous to health and the environment for as long as a half-million years, they are not really disposed of but must be stored using measures of security unprecedented in human history.

The search for a permanent storage site for spent nuclear fuel and other atomic garbage has resulted in some strange and fanciful proposals, from simply letting the stuff melt its way down into the Antarctic ice cap to stuffing it between the tectonic plates on the ocean floor and hoping it would disappear into the deepest maw of all. Most proposals have been more prosaic, however, consisting of deep holes bored into the ground at places located as far as possible from people—both to protect public health and to avoid political problems—and in geological formations that are as stable as possible. Five hundred thousand years is a long time. Earthquakes and other major perturbations are to be avoided.

The search centered on out-of-the-way places. Places like the Hanford Reservation in eastern Washington, Deaf Smith County in east Texas, the federal bombing range in Nevada, the desert near Carlsbad, New Mexico, and the badlands of southern Utah. No site for a nuclear waste dump will please everyone. The Utah sites (two were suggested) pleased almost no one, since they were right on the border of Canyonlands National Park, in canyons that should and one day might be inside the park.

When the list of candidate sites was released, the Legal Defense Fund—along with many other slickrock lovers— protested. All were unhappy at the prospect of a nuclear waste dump on the border of Canyonlands National Park, much as they had been displeased at the prospect of a stripmine on the outskirts of Bryce Canyon. But there was no handy law under which to petition for a declaration that Johnson Canyon and Lavender Canyon were unsuitable for an atomic garbage dump, and Tony Ruckel and other staff attorneys worried that aesthetic arguments might not win the day in court.

They decided to examine closely the technical aspects of this project, and discovered that the nuclear garbagemen had utterly ignored the work of the geologist most familiar with the area, Dr. Robert Huntoon of the University of Wyoming. Through many years of study, Dr. Huntoon had made two findings that cast serious doubt on the advisability of the plan to bury radioactive waste on the eastern flank of Canyonlands. One had to do with the way the Madison limestone salt formation beneath the canyons had been laid down. The Department of Energy said it tilted south and ended 200 miles away in the Grand Canyon. Therefore should there be an escape of radiation, it would have to migrate 200 miles before it would reach daylight, and that would take so long that it wouldn't be dangerous by the time it escaped. Dr. Huntoon said, on the contrary, that the limestone discharged into Dark Canyon

of the Colorado River scarcely twenty-five miles from the park. Thus, radiation escaping into groundwater would contaminate the outside world eight times sooner, more or less, than the government had calculated in making its recommendation.

Dr. Huntoon's second argument also involved the Madison limestone salt. He found that it was "overpressured," which could allow escaped radiation to reach the surface or to contaminate groundwater beneath the formation quite rapidly.

Ruckel immediately retained Dr. Huntoon and took him to Washington, D.C., to talk to the appropriate officials in the Environmental Protection Agency and the Department of Energy. Following those meetings, the Canyonlands sites were dropped from the list of repository candidates.

Many of these disputes—dams, mines, powerplants, and the like—have had two distinct lines of debate. First is the resource itself and how its utilization would affect the countryside. The other—the part that caused effigy burnings and encouraged most of the politicians and citizens of Utah to support the development projects—was the urge to bring jobs and economic growth to the area.

Ironically, in order to protect Grand Canyon from proposed hydroelectric dams, conservationists suggested plants fueled by coal and uranium. Then, to save the land and the skies from coal and uranium development, they began to suggest tourism as a more benign way to bring jobs and dollars to the region. What they had in mind was the sort of tourists who camp in national parks and run rivers in rubber rafts. What they got was a proposal by Garfield County, Utah, to pave the Burr Trail, a dirt track that winds sixty-odd miles from Boulder, Utah, through Capitol Reef National Park, to the shore of Lake Powell.

The land traversed by the Burr Trail is much like the places in Capitol Reef and Canyonlands, and it's likely that the two wilderness study areas flanking the trail would themselves be a national park were it not for so much gorgeous scenery nearby. Tourism boosters saw a gold mine waiting to be dug—and how better to reap a rich harvest than with a new, improved, widened, flattened, smoothed-out road to zip people from their motels at Boulder (soon to be built) to their speedboats and houseboats on Lake Powell (soon to be available for rent or lease)?

Conservationists were appalled. The Burr Trail was handy to provide access to some wild and remote washes and gullies, and it forced a slow pace of travel ideally suited to that country. The would-be pavers asked Congress to underwrite the considerable cost of their project, and Congress refused, not once but several times, citing the environmental delicacy of the area. The pavers would not take no for an answer. In the spring of 1987, they announced that the state of Utah was going to spend some federal dollars meant for emergency projects of one sort or another to get the project underway. They hired a bulldozer team to begin the job. The Bureau of Land Management, which controls most of the road outside the national park, sat on its hands. Lori Potter, Legal Defense Fund staff attorney in Denver, filed suit.

The Watchman and the Virgin River, Zion National Park.

The judge told the county to call off the bulldozers while he considered the matters in the case. After a lengthy hearing he ruled, finding that the pavers had to take some protective steps but giving them most of what they wanted. Again the bulldozers were fired up, and again Potter went to court, this time because the pavers had neglected to perform measurements and studies the court had ruled they must carry out before proceeding. She also appealed the substance of the case to the Court of Appeals in Denver. Again the 'dozers were stopped.

The legal issue in the case — and in numerous other cases past, present, and, no doubt, future — revolved around Revised Statute number 2477, a nineteenth-century law that guaranteed rights-of-way across federal lands to states, counties, and individuals if they could prove the existence of old roads or trails that had been used to reach mining claims. Burr Trail was, according to the pavers, an RS2477 road and therefore available to Garfield County for improvement despite the fact that the law had been repealed in 1976.

The final outcome of the Burr Trail litigation was a mixed bag, and suggests that RS2477 will continue to plague public lands for some time to come. The Tenth Circuit Court of Appeals ruled that Garfield County does have a right-of-way to the Burr Trail, but only to the current roadway — it cannot widen or move the route without express permission from the Bureau of Land Management. And further, as part of the negotiations between the parties, the improved road will avoid an especially sensitive canyon where upgrading the road would ruin a stream and nearby marshes. Still, that wild part of Utah between the Aquarius Plateau and the shores of Lake Powell will soon be a little less wild, a little more crowded — although not nearly so tame and crowded as it would have become without the litigation.

The battle for the Southwest — which will continue as long as there's coal in the ground, water in the streams, and greed in human hearts — has been a rowdy, disorganized affair, with hundreds of players, scores of skirmishes, and many heroes. Without taking anything away from any of them, it clearly can be said that Legal Defense Fund lawyers played a pivotal role in keeping the region as free as it is from developments that ranged from the merely irritating to the downright disastrous.

CHAPTER FOUR

Redwood National Park
Of Chainsaws, a Slug, and a Worm

The Redwood National Park created by Congress and President Lyndon Johnson in 1968 was one of the odder pieces of real estate ever bestowed on the American public. It was in six separate pieces, three administered by the state of California, the rest by the National Park Service. It meandered down the coast for forty miles. Half the acreage in the new park was already protected as state parks. The major acquisition of private land for the park was the southernmost parcel, which was shaped like a giant fly swatter. It is the handle of that fly swatter—widely known as "the worm"—that is the main concern of this narrative.

Ancient ancestors of the tree we now call the coast redwood, *sequoia sempervirens,* once blanketed the temperate zones of North America, Europe, and Asia. A slowly changing climate nearly doomed the giant trees, leaving only a narrow coastal strip that, at the beginning of the twentieth century, stretched more or less unbroken from the Big Sur south of Monterey to the southernmost reaches of Oregon, a fringe approximately 400 miles long. Far smaller populations of two other subspecies survive as well, the *sequoia gigantea* or giant sequoia of the southern Sierra Nevada and the *matasequoia glyptostroboides* or dawn redwood of China.

The coast redwoods made their last stand on the coast not least because of the weather, and particularly because of the fog. They seem also to have a

Clearing fog in the Tall Trees Grove, Redwood National Park, California.

competitive advantage over other tree species in their ability to withstand periodic flooding and occasional fires. In all these respects, the redwoods and the hills and valleys of the north coast were ideally suited to each other, and the trees grew taller than any others on Earth. When logging of the coast redwoods began in earnest in the nineteenth century, there were reports of trees as tall as 450 feet.

By the middle of the twentieth century, when the campaign for a Redwood National Park moved into high gear, the tallest remaining *sequoia sempervirens*—an 800-year-old tree that reached more than 365 feet into the sky—stood on a broadly curved alluvial flat next to Redwood Creek, the handle of the fly swatter.

How Redwood National Park came to look as it did for the first ten years of its existence is the result of the unusual and tumultuous circumstances surrounding its creation. When the idea of a national park to preserve redwoods was first suggested in the 1880s, it would have been relatively painless to create, because the federal government still had considerable holdings in the redwood country. By the turn of the century, however, most of the public land had been homesteaded, claimed by private owners who soon sold their interests to lumber companies. Whereas the vast majority of the national parks have been set aside from lands already owned by the federal government, any national park in the redwoods would have to be bought. In those days, however, the redwood empire must have seemed too vast to be vanquished. A national park could wait.

By the second decade of this century, the plight of the redwoods was all too obvious. There were sawmills in nearly every watershed in redwood country, and the giants were falling in droves. In 1919 a group of influential men met in San Francisco and formed the Save the Redwoods League. Their aim was to save spectacular groves of trees, many along roadsides to protect views. Little attention was paid at this stage to preserving entire watersheds.

The league acquired substantial tracts of virgin redwoods and turned them over to the state of California for management as state parks. The league's leaders—mainly Republicans from old and distinguished families—were not by nature enthusiastic about the federal government. They were especially wary of Franklin Roosevelt and the New Deal. The league resisted an attempt in the 1930s to create a redwood national park.

By the 1960s, however, the league came to support the creation of a national park in the redwoods. The Sierra Club shared the league's goal, but the two organizations were sponsoring very different proposals and the competition between them was not always polite. The league's preferred site was in Mill Creek, a watershed between Jedediah Smith and Del Norte Redwood state parks. The Sierra Club, meanwhile, was pushing for acquisition of the Redwood Creek drainage, a far larger section that provided the opportunity to preserve an entire redwood ecosystem, from the ocean to the inland ridgetops. The National Park Service had endorsed the Redwood Creek site in the early 1960s, but switched to Mill Creek midway through

the decade. The state of California—Ronald Reagan was then governor—was officially unenthusiastic about the whole idea but willing to talk about deals, such as not objecting to a national park as long as the Mineral King ski resort could be built (more on this in Chapter One).

Americans have a fondness for superlatives; it would be only natural to preserve the tallest trees in the whole wide world. But the Sierra Club's support for Redwood Creek was based as much on ecological concepts as on vertical feet. The Club argued forcefully—in the halls of Congress and in full-page newspaper ads—that the league's approach of buying only the finest groves of trees should be expanded to acquisition of an entire watershed, so that the park would not be harmed by activities upslope and upstream from it. There was ample evidence that such harm could occur.

Some say that the finest grove of redwoods ever to exist was astride Bull Creek, a tributary of the south fork of the Eel River. Thousands of 300-foot-tall trees flanked the stream, and salmon and steelhead swarmed in the creek at spawning time. In 1931, 8,000 acres of the best bottomland was acquired by the state through the generosity of the Rockefellers and others, via the Save the Redwoods League. It was named Humboldt Redwoods State Park, and the Bull Creek flats christened the Rockefeller Grove. The 20,000 acres upslope and upstream from the park, however, remained in private hands.

In 1947 the owners began logging the hillsides above the state park in earnest. The hillsides were steep and composed of an unstable soil similar to what hugs the slopes above Redwood Creek. Bulldozers slashed roads across these tremulous slopes, chainsaws tore into the flesh of the mighty trees, and tractors shoved and hauled the fallen trunks to waiting logging trucks. By 1954 more than half the watershed had been clearcut, and the hillsides began slowly making their way down into Bull Creek, silting in spawning beds, darkening crystal waters. A series of fires burned away slash and shrubs that had begun to recolonize the denuded slopes.

Then came the winter of 1955–56, a ferocious one. Torrents of rain washed down the ravaged hillsides and formed a deadly, gritty battering ram that tore away the banks of Bull Creek, undercutting the giant redwoods on the banks. That one winter, an estimated 420 trees more than 300 feet tall fell in a tumbled heap. In subsequent years more fell. In the late 1950s, the state acquired the rest of the watershed and began the difficult job of restoring it. It will be five hundred or a thousand years before Bull Creek regains its former glory.

Redwood Creek was another matter. Though much of the upper reaches of the watershed had been logged, the lower half remained fairly intact into the 1960s. The Sierra Club, led by Martin Litton, Edgar Wayburn, Mike McCloskey, and Dave Brower, argued that in order to preclude a replay of Bull Creek at Redwood Creek, the whole drainage should be acquired, from ridgeline to ridgeline.

The park created in 1968 was about as far from that ideal as it could possibly have been. If a camel is a horse designed by a committee, Redwood National Park was a preserve

Lower Redwood Creek, Redwood National Park. Erosion from logging has made the gravel beds wider than they would naturally be.

Meadow of daisies and grasses along Redwood Creek.

Stinging nettles along Redwood Creek.

designed by the United Nations on a day when all the interpreters called in sick. It encompassed, as mentioned above, three state parks, a smidgen of Mill Creek, a few slices of connective tissue, and an oddly shaped dollop of Redwood Creek. The northern section was fine — it ran from ridge to ridge along the last few miles of Redwood Creek before it empties into the Pacific. But upstream from that was the infamous "worm," an eight-mile-long, half-mile-wide corridor that extended from the main part of the park upstream to just past Tall Trees Grove. The worm was created in an effort to protect part of an unmatched expanse of streamside giants called the Emerald Mile, but the omission of the upper slopes along the corridor seemed guaranteed to lead to another Bull Creek disaster.

Celebrations of the new park reflected more relief than joy. The long struggle was over, but the result satisfied no one. The league got a little of Mill Creek, the Sierra Club got a little of Redwood Creek, and the American people got a truncated and terribly vulnerable national park. There simply wasn't enough money to acquire all the land both organizations wanted. Some discretion was left to the Interior Department about precise boundaries: Congress said it wanted not more than 58,000 acres and it wanted to spend no more than $92 million.

In the last several months before the park legislation was approved, Arcata Redwood and Simpson Timber Company voluntarily suspended logging in several areas that were being considered for acquisition, including the slopes above the worm. (Georgia Pacific, the other major landowner in the area, refused to stop cutting, and offered a mind-twisting defense of clearcutting in that rugged country. "The large old-growth heavy timber should be removed," intoned the company, "to reduce the threat of slides and erosion.") After the bill was signed, Arcata and Simpson tore into the trees with everything they had, probably knowing that attempts would be mounted to enlarge the park or to restrict cutting near the park. And that is precisely what happened.

Once it became clear that cutting was being accelerated near the park boundaries, and after informal requests to the National Park Service to take steps to protect the park had been ignored, the Sierra Club Legal Defense Fund filed a formal petition in September 1971, demanding that the Interior Department take control of 47,000 acres adjacent to the park. The Legal Defense Fund based its petition on a crucial paragraph in the law that created the park, a paragraph that made it clear that Congress was well aware of the possible dangers the park would face from outside its margins. The law said this:

Rhododendron, Lady Bird Johnson Grove, Redwood National Park.

Pacific fog cloaks trees in the Redwood Creek watershed, with the coastline in the far distance.

Drifted redwood snag along Redwood Creek. It lies on the immense gravel "slug" created by logging.

In order to afford as full protection as is reasonably possible to the timber, soil and streams within the boundaries of the park, the Secretary of Interior is authorized . . . to acquire interests in land from, and to enter into contracts and cooperative agreements with, the owners of land on the periphery of the park and on watersheds tributary to streams within the park, designed to assure that the consequences of forest management, timbering, land use and soil conservation practices conducted thereon, or of the lack of such practices, will not adversely affect the timber, soil and streams within the park.

The Interior Department, in the hallowed style of governments everywhere, decided to appoint a task force to look into the matter. The members of the task force visited the park and its surroundings in the spring of 1972. In the fall, Sierra Club leaders were told that a task force report had been written. Their request for copies of the report was ignored, and after repeated requests also went unanswered, John Hoffman, staff attorney for the Legal Defense Fund, filed suit under the Freedom of Information Act. It was March 1973.

Rather than defend a patently indefensible position, the Interior Department promptly issued the report, but before doing so it lopped off the last two pages. These pages contained a number of recommendations, including a suggestion that the government buy 1,650 acres as a buffer around the worm. Director James T. Lynn of the Office of Management and Budget vetoed the suggestion as too expensive, proving that David Stockman wasn't the first Scrooge to occupy that position. The existence of the recommendations became known only during subsequent litigation.

The report itself, written by Dr. Richard C. Curry of the Interior Department, confirmed conservationists' fears. Redwood Creek was rapidly being degraded owing to erosion from old clearcuts far south in the watershed, to the zealous cutting then going on adjacent to the park, and to nature itself.

Surface erosion and landslides had already added millions of cubic yards of sand, gravel, and silt to the beds of Redwood Creek and its tributaries, forming what the researchers called a giant "slug." This was moving slowly downstream, widening the streambed, eroding the banks, and undercutting streamside vegetation. Some kind of action was urgently needed, but the government seemed unwilling to make a move. The Legal Defense Fund amended its lawsuit, asking the court to order the Park Service to take immediate steps to rescue Redwood Creek.

The government responded that it had neither power nor authority to do anything about activities taking place outside the park and asked that the suit be dismissed. It also refused to acknowledge that the logging outside the park was the principal cause of current and anticipated damage to the park.

The case was assigned to Judge William T. Sweigert, who still had the Mineral King case on his docket. Responding to preliminary motions from the government to dismiss the case, Judge Sweigert, in the first of three written opinions he would issue in the case, brushed off the government's excuses, finding not only that the quoted paragraph in the Redwood Park law gave the government authority to protect the park but also that there was a "general fiduciary responsibility" on the part of the Interior Department to safeguard the national parks for the people of the United States. John Hoffman at that point became Executive Director of the Legal Defense Fund; he turned the case over to Michael Sherwood, a new staff attorney whose background included Stanford Law School and several years of legal practice in Hawaii.

Sherwood rounded up a team of experts and made a visit to the scene of the cutting. There was Gordon Robinson, a gentle soul of deep moral conviction, who had served as the principal forester with the Southern Pacific Railroad for many years and then retired to become a consultant; he was on the staff of the Sierra Club. Bob Curry made the trip too. Curry is a renowned geologist and geomorphologist, and brilliant in many other fields as well. At the time he was employed by the Club in a short-lived research department. They collected Dave Van de Mark as they drove through Trinidad, California, on their way north. Van de Mark, a photographer, had been visiting Redwood Creek for ten years, making by his estimate several hundred trips to the area. He was a leading proponent of including Redwood Creek in the park and would act as guide.

"I guess it's safe to admit now that we may have trespassed a bit on private land," Sherwood recalled years later. "Unfortunately, that was the only way to see firsthand what was going on. It was a war zone. Stumps everywhere, land scraped bare of all cover. The noise was the worst—the incessant whine and snarl of chainsaws, the grumble and roar of bulldozers, the thud of giant redwoods crashing down. The ground shook. We all knew what to expect, but we were shaken anyway. It was an ugly, brutal sight. Gordon said it was the most abusive clearcutting he'd ever seen."

The trial commenced in Judge Sweigert's courtroom in San Francisco on May 20, 1975. Just as the Disney organization had stayed out of the Mineral King litigation, the timber companies chose not to intervene in this case, but that didn't keep them from attending the trial, where their representatives filled most of the seats.

Mike Sherwood squared off against Paul Locke of the U.S. Attorney's office, but Judge Sweigert took an unusually active role right from the outset. He questioned witnesses extensively, advised the attorneys on how to structure their arguments, scolded them for straying from what he thought the line of questioning should be. He comes across as slightly brusque in a reading of the trial transcript, but not without a sense of humor. If he made life difficult for Sherwood, he made it miserable for Locke.

Dave Van de Mark testified first. He told the court he'd seen thousand-acre clearcuts in the Redwood Creek drainage, and that the rate of cutting had accelerated as soon as the park bill became law. Sherwood had enlarged some of Van de Mark's most telling photographs, showing clearcuts right up to the skin of the worm in some places. Van de Mark's commentary was vivid: "I stood on the bank of this stream that is flowing chocolate, absolutely sapped goo. You can hear materials slopping and slipping off into this watershed."

Richard Janda, a geologist for the U.S. Geological Survey, came next. Sweigert was, shall we say, abrupt.

Judge Sweigert asked Dr. Janda to list his observations, "so I can write them down."

JANDA: There are a series of values in Redwood National Park . . .
JUDGE: Don't use the word values.
JANDA: There are aquatic resources.
JUDGE: Just a minute. Come down to earth. Now. What's going on in the park that you can see? Please tell me, one, two, three, four.

Janda described how erosion increases and threatens the trees and ruins the fishery.

JUDGE: Is there any relation of cause and effect between those conditions and what's going on outside?
JANDA: It's difficult to establish any direct cause and effect with regard to present logging.
JUDGE: Just answer the question first and explain later. Would you say there is any relation of cause and effect between the things that are occurring in and around the main channel which you have described on the one hand and those logging timber operations on the other?
JANDA: Indeed, Your Honor, there is some cause and effect relationship. It's difficult to quantify it.
JUDGE: No matter how difficult it is, if there is something, what is it?
JANDA: The accelerated erosion from cut-over land, I believe, is responsible for the introduction of sediment to the creek, which has caused the filling of pools to change the character of the spawning gravels, the erosion of the stream banks and the various problems that I spelled out earlier.

And finally the judge had the answer he wanted.

Bob Curry testified next and reinforced what Janda had said. He said the only way to save the park was to stop the logging and reforest all the cutover land in the entire watershed, ninety percent of which had been cut by the time the trial was held. He called for a "sediment management plan" to keep an eye on the slug and try to figure out some way to stop it from gnawing disastrously at the tall trees.

Then Gordon Robinson took the stand. "He had a shock of white hair like Judge Sweigert did," Sherwood recalled, "and they hit it off immediately. I asked one or two questions, then the judge took over. Gordon swung his chair so that he was facing the judge, and they just had a one-on-one conversation. The rest of us were spectators."

Robinson told the sad history of redwood logging—of how the original 2,000,000 acres of old growth had been reduced to 150,000, of how nearly half the old growth in the Redwood Creek drainage outside the park had been cut in the seven years following the creation of the park. He described his view of how forests ought to be managed, cutting only as much year by year as the forest can produce, forever. Early in his career,

Robinson had convinced the Southern Pacific Railroad not to sell its forest lands as it was planning to do, but rather to manage them for timber production without clearcutting, without cutting too much too fast. The railroad earned a modest profit, something latter-day timber companies tend to say is impossible. Robinson said he knew of no reason why so-called sustained-yield selection management wouldn't work in old-growth redwood forests. It not only makes sense in the abstract, it has the added advantages of minimizing insect damage and fire hazards, it produces better timber, and it's nicer to look at.

Clearcutting—the management scheme most favored in the redwoods and many other places—is the worst way to practice forestry, Robinson told the court. Roading, yarding, and felling of trees compacts the soil. Melting snow and rain are less able to seep into the ground and run off all in a rush. This causes immediate erosion and later deprives the soil of water that otherwise is held in a natural subsurface reservoir. It leads to forests where all the trees are the same age and size, which increases vulnerability to insects and blight.

The judge then questioned Robinson closely on his recommendations for improving the situation in Redwood Creek. Robinson told the court that logging should begin at the ridgetop and proceed down, to protect the stream. He said that timber removal should be limited to that amount that could be harvested at the same rate forever.

Much of the conversation at this stage in the trial had to do with draft agreements that the National Park Service had been trying to reach between itself and Georgia (now Louisiana) Pacific, Arcata, and Simpson. The agency hoped it could persuade the companies to accept some restraints on their operations, rather than issuing regulations that would be subject to judicial challenge and that might be considered a "taking."

"Taking" is a frequent topic of dispute in environmental matters, particularly when the issue involves the regulation by government of activities carried out on private land by the owners of that land. The U.S. Constitution bars government from taking property without compensating its owners. Sometimes, depending on the circumstances, courts have found that government regulations prohibiting a landowner from carrying out certain economic activities on his property constitute an illegal taking. Government lawyers feared that if they told Simpson, Arcata, and Louisiana Pacific how much timber they could cut on their lands and how they must do it, the companies would sue. For that reason, they entered into long negotiations to reach what they called "cooperative agreements" with the companies.

At trial, the agreements were called by that name and a few others. Mike Sherwood led the charge. He pointed out that the agreements were not binding and, for that matter, that none had been signed except for Simpson's, which had been signed by the company but not by the government. Judge Sweigert was interested and somewhat perplexed. For the duration of the trial, the items were usually referred to as "proposed so-called cooperative agreements." It must have been difficult not to giggle.

Lupine on Counts Hill prairie, Redwood Creek watershed, Redwood National Park.

Grass tussocks in Redwood Creek.

Water-worn stones and reflected foliage in Redwood Creek.

The upper gorge of Redwood Creek, in the newer portion of the national park.

Sherwood and his witnesses punched hole after hole in the proposed so-called cooperative agreements. Gordon Robinson translated several passages of officious gobbledygook that turned out to have no force or effect. There was no limit on the size of clearcuts allowed by the agreements or on the amount of timber the companies could cut in a given period of time. The following exchange is typical:

SHERWOOD: Arcata intends to clearcut all the remaining virgin old-growth timber right up to the park boundary; isn't that correct?
GLENN REED (Arcata Redwood Company): Over a period of a great many years.
SHERWOOD: How many years?
REED: That depends on how these [agreements] are adopted.
SHERWOOD: How many years do these proposed harvesting guidelines envision?
REED: An absolute minimum of, I would say, ten to twelve.

Hardly a very long time. And even if the agreements had required selective cutting rather than clearcutting, it would not have made much difference:

SHERWOOD: Mr. Merrill, has your company done any selective cutting?
ALFRED MERRILL (Louisiana Pacific): Yes, we have. We still do.
SHERWOOD: What percentage cut do you make with your selective cutting?
MERRILL: We were customarily making a cut of thirty to thirty-five percent of the volume of the timber standing on the area in the old-growth stand. Often the percentage was higher because so many of the trees are defective and these trees aren't capable of adding any further growth; and it's customary to remove them in the harvest so the cut land ranges all the way from about sixty percent to eighty or ninety percent depending on the type of selective cutting that was carried out and the condition of the forest prior to the time of harvest operations.
SHERWOOD: That's what you would define as selective cutting, a technique removing up to ninety percent?
MERRILL: That's the technical [definition of] selective cutting in the redwood region.

As if that weren't bad enough, by provisions of the proposed so-called cooperative agreements, the company's foresters could override provisions of the agreements at will. The agreements could not be strengthened, only weakened. Merrill, Reed, and Henry Trobitz of Simpson Timber Company insisted that they fully intended to abide by the agreements but admitted under stiff questioning from Sherwood that they didn't have to. The government, meanwhile, said it could not sign the agreements without first producing an environmental impact statement on their effects, a process that had begun but would take many more months.

Finally, the government produced its star witness, the Assistant Secretary of the Interior for Fish, Wildlife and Parks, Nat Reed. Reed was a Floridian with good environmental credentials, whose job made him responsible for all the national parks and wildlife refuges. He had been flown in unexpectedly from Washington to save the government's case.

Reed did not admit or deny that Redwood National Park was being harmed by the logging on its perimeter, arguing that it was impossible to tell from the studies conducted thus far; more were underway. The problem, articulated by several witnesses, was that the admitted damage was the result of several factors, and it was difficult to separate the effects of the park-side logging from the others.

Reed conceded that Congress had told the Interior Department to take steps to protect the park through one of several methods. Reed's problem was that most of the money authorized for the park had been spent, and by the time all outstanding claims were settled, the Interior Department would have spent more than twice as much as Congress had authorized. He couldn't see buying more land outright, or leasing it, or acquiring easements without new funds. This is what the Curry report had recommended, but the Office of Management and Budget had refused to let Interior ask Congress for more money. In any case, Reed wanted to await the results of yet another study of the situation, this being carried out by Richard Janda, one of Mike Sherwood's witnesses.

Sherwood asked if Mr. Reed weren't taking a "calculated risk" by waiting for the results of the Janda study. "I believe we are taking a calculated risk," admitted Reed. He also revealed that the Interior Department was contemplating asking the Justice Department to sue the logging companies for bringing harm to the park. In the end, Reed told the court that his hands were tied; he was powerless. Congress had indeed told the department to protect the park but hadn't given it the power to do so.

Judge Sweigert then wrote the second of his three opinions, in July of 1975. He ruled that the park was indeed being damaged by logging on private land nearby and that the government was failing in its duty to protect the park. He didn't impose any penalty or issue any specific orders, however, except to tell the government to do *something* and to report back to him its progress within 150 days.

The chainsaws, meanwhile, kept on sinking their teeth into trees that began life hundreds of years before there was a United States of America, an American judicial system, or a National Park Service.

Five months later the Interior Department filed a progress report with the court, just as vague as its previous statements and documents. It was working with the logging companies, the agency said. It was contemplating various legal and legislative remedies. In a separate report to Congress, however, the department reversed its long-held position and conceded that the park was being damaged and that its previous practices were insufficient to protect the park. Mike Sherwood objected to the report filed with the court, and asked the judge to find that the department was in contempt of the July order.

As the judge was considering that request, the Interior Department issued a final report to the court, in February 1976. In that report, it told the court it intended to propose

Coastal redwoods and ground cover, Redwood National Park.

legislation that would give the Interior Secretary direct authority to regulate logging outside the park. A nuisance suit against the timber companies had been requested from the Department of Justice as well, the agency reported. In sum, it was doing all it could do.

The litigation and its attendant publicity had kicked up a storm of public protest, and Congress—led by California Democrats Phillip Burton and Leo Ryan—was making noises about once again taking matters into its own hands. Conservationists, led by the Sierra Club, renewed their struggle to persuade Congress to expand the park.

Judge Sweigert issued his final ruling in the case on June 7, 1976. He pronounced himself satisfied that, under the circumstances, the Interior Department had done and was doing all it could to protect the park. At the same time he acknowledged that the park was in desperate peril and that something should be done. That something, however, would have to be done by Congress. It was beyond the power of the courts to direct Congress to spend money or to tell the Office of Management and Budget to ask for it. The judge's opinion was an impassioned plea to Congress to save the national park it had created and left so vulnerable.

The Legal Defense Fund did not appeal the decision, but turned its efforts to the legislative campaign to enlarge the park. Mike Sherwood flew to Washington three months later to testify before Congressman Ryan's subcommittee on conservation, energy, and natural resources. He recited the history of the litigation, stressing that the park was in grave danger and urging that new legislation be passed quickly to set matters right. The lawyers had reached the end of their road, he told the lawmakers, now only you can save Redwood National Park.

During the two years that followed, the debate in Congress and in the press had as much to do with jobs as it did with clearcutting and erosion. Loggers, fearful of losing their jobs, banded together to block expansion of the park, at one point sending a convoy of twenty-three big rigs to Washington to ring the White House. One of them carried an eight-ton redwood peanut to greet the new president, Jimmy Carter. The rest bore the trunks of giant old-growth redwoods.

Eventually a compromise was struck, through the legislative skill of Congressman Phillip Burton. The park was nearly doubled: 48,000 acres were added to the original 58,000 and an upstream buffer zone of 30,000 acres was designated, within which the Park Service had authority to comment on timber-harvest plans and to acquire additional lands if necessary. The price tag was bigger than any previous federal land acquisition—for a park or any other purpose—in American history: an estimated $360 million or more. Thirty-three million dollars was authorized for the rehabilitation of the Redwood Creek drainage. In addition, there was a complicated package of benefits for loggers who would lose their jobs—retraining, Park Service employment in restoring the new parkland, and direct payments. Labor benefits in the bill were estimated eventually to total at least $40 million. Nothing like it had ever been done before.

The most expensive national park in the nation's history was also the most severely wounded. Of the 48,000 acres added to the original park, 9,000 were virgin old growth; the rest had been logged. In the park as a whole, only about one-fifth of the land the federal government obtained from the timber companies held virgin forest. Redwood National Park was a rehabilitation project of gigantic proportions, and an expensive one at that.

Twenty years after the park was created, ten years after it was expanded, the restoration of Redwood Creek is well underway. Of the 250 or so miles of logging roads that once scarred the hillsides and led to so much damage, all but about 75 have been put to bed, as they say, although some of what's left will be kept for the convenience of park visitors. Logging debris has been removed from miles of tributary streams. Rainy-season creeks have been returned to their original courses, sometimes with the help of riprap, most often not. The Park Service has planted three quarters of a million trees since 1978. The practice is to plant small, bare-root redwoods and Douglas firs, then to let the alders invade, as they will after fires or avalanches—or clearcuts—in that country. The alders are nitrogen-fixers, and will thus help restore the soil as the conifers inch upward. After about forty years, the firs and redwoods will shade out the alders. A hundred years later, make that two hundred, the devastated land will once again deserve to be called "old growth."

Most of the physical restoration of the watershed is now complete—at least the part that can be done by men. Park Service scientists like John Sacklin, a young "environmental specialist" who has assisted with rehabilitation work since 1978, now debate more philosophical questions, such as whether it would be a good idea to thin out the stands of second-growth redwoods now growing so densely on the older clearcuts.

As for the biggest trees down in the creek bottom, there's still that slug, sliding slowly down the creek toward the sea. In the mid-1980s, a series of storms, combined with the hydrological mischief the slug gets the creek into, brought Redwood Creek to within ten or fifteen feet of the base of the sixth tallest tree in the world, a perilously short distance. As soon as the flood subsided, the Park Service took the drastic step of sending a bulldozer up the streambed from Orick to the Tall Trees Grove. It shoved some gravel and sand back up against the slope where it belonged—where it would have been were it not for the slug. "I doubt if we'd do that again," John Sacklin said later. "Our approach now is to let nature take its course."

And nature will. In its own good time, given the eleventh-hour reprieve from relentless logging, nature will put Redwood Creek back together again. It makes one want to believe in reincarnation, John Sacklin agreed as he proudly showed off a new trail through the Tall Trees Grove. "I just wish I could come back here in five hundred or a thousand years and see how well we did."

Birds, Beasts, and Bedfellows
The Fight for Endangered Species

It is popular—and appropriate—to lament man's behavior toward the creatures he shares the planet with: beastly, one might be forgiven for calling it. But despite, or maybe because of, the tragic history that has led to the decimation of so many species and the extinction of so many others, there has crept into law the most uncompromising protection for endangered species. It is as strong as the protection for any class of beings, from schoolchildren to welfare mothers, from racial minorities to starving artists.

It must have something to do with the finality of extinction, with the horror of knowing that once the last individual of a species is gone, it is gone forever. With extinction there is no turning back, no second chance, no instant replay to see who should be penalized. It is final in a way that few things are final.

For that reason and others, the strongest environmental law in the American system of laws is the Endangered Species Act of 1973. Unlike anti-pollution laws, or laws that govern the Forest Service and the National Park Service, or

*Palila (*Loxioides bailleui*), Big Island of Hawaii. By Jack Jeffrey, U.S. Fish and Wildlife Service.*

even the National Environmental Policy Act itself, the Endangered Species Act permits almost no compromise. Species deemed by the best scientific studies to be in peril for their existence are protected absolutely. With extremely rare exceptions, nothing can be permitted that will jeopardize them or their chance of recovering to a population of stable size.

The law specifically prohibits the "taking" of endangered species, and defines "take" to mean "harass, harm, pursue, hunt, shoot, wound, kill, trap, capture, or collect."

The law is tough and unyielding. Enforcement of it, however, as with many other environmental laws, has not always been as vigorous as Congress clearly intended and the public has repeatedly demanded. The Legal Defense Fund first hefted this potent weapon in 1978, on behalf of a small, yellow-headed Hawaiian bird called the palila.

Habitat for a Honeycreeper

Some Hawaiian natural scientists suggest that the only reason Charles Darwin didn't adduce his theory of evolution on Hawaii is that he stumbled onto the Galápagos Islands first. There may be something to what they say. The Hawaiian Islands are farther from any mainland than the Galápagos, and so, for many years, were even more insulated from outside influences.

Like other remote islands, they have evolved unique communities of life, with hundreds of species that exist nowhere else. Endemic, they're called. For their size, the Hawaiian Islands have more unique species than anywhere else on Earth, and each island is different from the others in the species that evolved and live there.

Despite this plethora of species, the Hawaiian Islands—like many in the Pacific Ocean—all but skipped mammals, concentrating instead on a spectacular assortment of plants, birds, insects, and mollusks. There are monk seals and other indigenous marine mammals offshore and hoary bats onshore, but there are no other native terrestrial mammals. No mice, no deer, no skunks. No raccoons, no buffalo, no giraffes. And, until a millennium or so ago, no people.

When the first people did come, Pacific islanders from the south and west, they brought with them pigs, dogs, rats, and chickens, which got loose or were set loose on the unprotected islands to prosper and multiply, which they did. The native trees and shrubs, having evolved without the need to cope with grazing or browsing animals, were at a distinct disadvantage. They had no thorns to discourage nibblers, no noxious sap to repel ungulates or rodents. The animals, for their part, had no natural enemies in their new home, so they found it easy to get established and begin an eventual population explosion.

When the first people arrived in the Hawaiian Archipelago, it must have been like stepping inside the world's biggest exotic bird shop. The skies and forests were thronged with gaudily colored birds of all sizes and shapes. So numerous were they that the king employed a whole corps of bird hunters to supply feathers to adorn his costumes and the necklines of his family and friends. It is reported that a ceremonial cloak worn by King Kamehameha I contained feathers from 80,000 birds of the species called *mamo.*. Leis, now made of orchids and other tropical flowers, were originally made with feathers. In many cases the birds died to serve the fashion whims of the Hawaiians; you don't shear a parrot the way you do a sheep.

As devastating as hunting was to native flora and fauna, the conversion of habitat to human purposes was even worse. Agriculture meant clearing land of its native cover in order to plant taro, bananas, sugar cane, breadfruit, coconut, and sweet potatoes. Nor did matters improve when European missionaries arrived following Captain Cook's "discovery" of the islands in 1778. They brought goats, sheep, and cattle and set them loose in the land; they too thrived. The native species never stood a chance. By the mid-twentieth century it was estimated that fully one-third of Hawaii's native species of birds had been extirpated, mainly because of agricultural usurpation of habitat and the introduction of exotic species. Most of those remaining were in danger of following the same path, as were many species of plants, insects, and mollusks.

Hawaii was not the only place where endemic species were in decline, of course, only the most prominent. By the mid-1960s, Congress had taken notice of the problem, passing a series of three laws, each stronger than the last, that led finally to the Endangered Species Act of 1973.

The act is supposed to work as follows: Once a species is found to be in serious decline, the U.S. Fish and Wildlife Service or the National Marine Fisheries Service may propose that it be listed. Public comments and further expert opinion are often solicited. At the end of some months or years—and occasionally more quickly if the situation is deemed an emergency—the Office of Endangered Species decides whether or not to add the species in question to the list.

In some circumstances citizens have taken matters into their own hands and lodged petitions with one agency or the other, asking that a species be added to the list. The agency then has a certain prescribed time in which to decide whether or not to list the species and to justify its decision. The agencies are allowed discretion in such judgment calls, and courts have not shown much interest in second-guessing them. In the late 1980s, however, conservationists have had some success in litigation aimed at forcing a reluctant agency to list species it didn't want to, a subject we shall get to presently.

Once a species is listed, the agency is required to designate its "critical habitat," the area that must be preserved and restored to ensure the survival and recovery of the species. Then it must write a "recovery plan" that outlines what the agency actually will do to ensure survival and recovery.

The first Endangered Species Preservation Act, passed in 1966, set up the list of threatened and endangered species. Of the first thirty-six birds put on the list, twenty were endemic to Hawaii. The palila, *loxioides bailleui,* a member of the honeycreeper group within the finch family, was one. The species lives only on the slopes of Mauna Kea, the highest mountain on the island and the state of Hawaii, between the elevations of 6,500 and 9,300 feet. Its range and population were much larger in historic times, but in the late 1970s this band around Mauna Kea was all that was left to sustain between 1,400 and 1,600 birds.

An adult palila is about six inches from end to end. Its back is grey, its abdomen whitish, its head a bright yellow. Its beak is broad, hooked, and short. It is about as unadventurous an eater as any in the bird kingdom, subsisting almost exclusively on the pods, flowers, seeds, and shoots of the mamane tree, an evergreen with grey-green foliage and yellow flowers that resemble some species of acacia. The birds not only feed on the mamane, they also build their nests in the trees, and occasionally in naio trees that grow in association with mamane on the flanks of the mountain. The palila's only known food other than mamane is an insect that also lives only on the mamane tree. It is a very exclusive society. Without mamane forest, the palila would perish.

In the mid-1970s, the mamane-naio forest was rapidly disappearing down the throats of feral sheep and goats—domesticated species that had escaped to the wild—and wild mouflon sheep imported from the Mediterranean and released for hunters to pursue. Much damage had already been done. In the mid-1930s, scientists estimated that there were 40,000 feral sheep in the mamane forest, and another 30,000 feral goats. The mouflon sheep were introduced in 1954, and their population grew despite the hunting. The various sheep and goats could eat a far broader variety of vegetation, but to the eternal misfortune of the palila, they found mamane to their liking, especially the tender shoots and seedlings.

Mamane trees are thought to live as long as 500 years, and it takes twenty-five years for a seedling to reach sufficient size and maturity to provide food and shelter for the palila. Therefore, the sheep and goats could and did dramatically retard the natural regeneration of the forest as they munched their way through it, and soon the palila's numbers began to plummet.

By the mid-1970s, owing largely to hunting, which was managed by the state, there were only about 500 each of the feral goats and sheep, maintained by the state for the recreational pleasure of sport hunters. The forest was in terrible condition, and it was clear to scientists who had been studying the situation for years that if the sheep and goats weren't removed entirely, the forest, and the palila with it, was doomed.

The Fish and Wildlife Service established the palila's critical habitat in 1976 and appointed a team to write a recovery plan for the bird. A preliminary plan was issued for public comment in early 1977. It called for total removal of feral sheep and goats from the mamane-naio forest on Mauna Kea and further study of the impact of feral pigs and mouflon sheep.

Common murre (Uria aalge) perched on a rock, Farallon Islands. By Frans Lanting/Minden Pictures.

Dusky dolphin (Lagenorhynchus obscurus), *off the coast of Patagonia. By William Curtsinger/Photo Researchers, Inc.*

The final plan was issued that same August. The appendix contained copies of comments received from public and private agencies. The Audubon Society endorsed the plan. The Smithsonian's International Council for Bird Preservation endorsed the plan. The U.S. Forest Service, which was nominated to pay for future research, endorsed the plan.

The state of Hawaii came in with a split verdict. The Fish and Game Division of the Department of Land and Natural Resources approved the plan but the department's Forestry Division turned thumbs down: "This recovery plan cannot be implemented. The Board [of Land and Natural Resources] has stated that they will not approve the total removal of feral goats and sheep from Mauna Kea." The hunting lobby had found its champion.

Lynn Greenwalt, Director of the U.S. Fish and Wildlife Service, approved the plan anyway, in January 1978. Hawaii refused to cooperate. The animals, the state reasoned, weren't killing the little birds, and the hunters weren't, either. Habitat modification was a bit too abstract a cause for the state to understand—or to take the political heat for espousing.

Conservationists—and scientists both inside and outside government familiar with the palila—were aghast at the state's decision. Scientific opinion was unanimous on the point: remove the feral goats and sheep or lose the palila. The bird's

defenders made contact with the Legal Defense Fund's Michael Sherwood, who, before joining the organization, had worked for several years in Hawaii as a government prosecutor and had helped local conservationists with some legal matters. Was there any way the Legal Defense Fund could come to the aid of the palila and its forest?

Sherwood examined the facts in the case and interviewed the principal ornithologists familiar with the birds' plight. He combed the Endangered Species Act and other statutes. Eventually he suggested that it ought to be possible to persuade a court that allowing the degradation of habitat necessary for the survival of an endangered species should constitute "harm" to the species, and therefore constitute a "taking," which is illegal under the act. Certain language in regulations the Fish and Wildlife Service wrote to implement the law frowns on disruption of endangered species' habitat, but this provision had never been tested in court. Sherwood recommended giving it a try.

He came in with all guns blazing. Taking a leaf from Justice Douglas's celebrated dissent in the Mineral King case, Sherwood named the palila itself as the lead plaintiff in the case. It was joined by its "next friends," the Hawaii Audubon Society, the National Audubon Society, the Sierra Club, and Dr. Alan Ziegler, a palila researcher and head of the Division of

Vertebrate Zoology at the Bishop Museum in Honolulu. It is a sign of the changed atmosphere surrounding environmental litigation that by 1978, when the case was filed, this stretching of the rules of standing was neither challenged by the opposition nor remarked by the court.

Sherwood submitted lengthy affidavits from virtually every palila expert, not to mention authorities on the mouflon sheep and the mamane-naio ecosystem. They all agreed with the proposition that feral goats, feral sheep, and wild palila could not coexist for long in the wild forest on the Big Island of Hawaii. Sherwood argued that the important facts in the case were not in dispute. He asked the court to accept the facts as submitted and find that the state was plainly and simply in violation of the law, and to issue what's known as a summary judgment and skip the bother and expense of a trial.

The case was assigned to Judge Samuel King, who had no known record or tendencies in environmental cases. Judge King scheduled a hearing on the matter and, after listening carefully to the lawyers' arguments, found that Sherwood was right. The important facts were simply that the palila was an endangered species and that the state's maintaining feral sheep and goats in the birds' critical habitat was a taking under the Endangered Species Act and therefore illegal. On June 6, 1979, he issued a summary judgment in favor of the plaintiffs. Two months later, he issued a formal written order, giving the state two years to remove all feral sheep and goats permanently and to report its progress to him at six-month intervals.

It was the first time that habitat modification had been found by a court to be a violation of the Endangered Species Act. The ruling would add considerable muscle to efforts to preserve endangered species if it could be sustained.

The state of Hawaii appealed to the Ninth Circuit Court of Appeals and asked Judge King meanwhile to stay his removal order pending the outcome. Judge King refused. The state asked the Court of Appeals to stay Judge King's order, and the higher court refused as well. The deadline for the state's first progress report to Judge King was February 1, 1980. Nothing happened, undoubtedly because, as Sherwood's informants in Hawaii had told him, there was nothing to report. The state was simply ignoring the proper and legal order of a federal judge.

On April 22, Sherwood suggested that Judge King ask the state to produce a report or be found in contempt. The state hustled together a "Status Report" that admitted the population of sheep had actually risen by thirty percent in the previous twelve months—not the sort of progress the court had in mind. The state had failed, for unexplained reasons, to declare a year-round open hunting season on the sheep and goats as the court had ordered it to do. Judge King said that if his orders continued to be ignored he would take over the department himself.

The Court of Appeals heard arguments in the case in November 1980. Two months later it gave its full endorsement to Judge King's decision, calling it "thorough and insightful." It had no trouble accepting the important argument that wrecking an endangered species' habitat was just as bad as blowing it away with a shotgun. The sheep and goats must go.

The pro-hunting forces, however, would not give up easily. The Reagan team had just taken power in Washington, and talk of "environmental extremists" and "environmental radicals" was issuing from such formerly friendly precincts as the Department of the Interior and the Environmental Protection Agency. In the early 1980s, the Fish and Wildlife Service announced that it was going to revise its definition of "harm," as prohibited by the Endangered Species Act.

Following a full page of fine print as meaningless prelude, the Federal Register in June 1981 carried the following:

> "Harm" in the definition of "take" in the Act means an act or omission which injures or kills wildlife.

The agency explained that the clarification was necessary because, owing to the palila lawsuit, some courts might be led to believe that *all* habitat modification within an endangered species' habitat was illegal even if it posed no threat to the creature in question. The real story, however, was a crass attempt to strip endangered species of their right to a secure habitat.

Fortunately, the wildlife-protection community was alert and knew exactly what was in the wind. Three hundred twenty-eight individuals and organizations wrote to the service to comment on the proposed redefinition. Mike Sherwood said that the attempted redefinition was an unconstitutional attempt to overturn by administrative regulation a valid court opinion. He threatened to file suit if the regulation was adopted as written. Eventually the Interior Department revised its definition slightly, but it did "harm" no harm.

Meanwhile, scientists were gathering data on the impact the mouflon sheep were having on the mamane and naio trees. To the surprise of no one, their federally ordered study, published in 1982 by the Hawaii Department of Land and Natural Resources, found that the mouflon were at least as damaging to the trees, and therefore to the palila, as the feral sheep and goats. The palila was literally being squeezed out of its forest. Mouflon liked to sleep above tree line, then browse their way down the mountain. As a result, Mauna Kea's tree line was creeping downhill, making the mountain look more and more like Friar Tuck.

The authors of the mouflon study suggested gamely that a limited population of mouflon might be able to coexist with the palila, and proposed also the possibility of erecting a fence or fences to contain a supply of sheep to be managed for sport hunting.

Sherwood jumped back into the ring. He reminded the Department of the first palila case—as if the agency could have forgotten—and asked that the mouflon, along with some remaining feral sheep and goats, be removed from the palila's range forthwith. The state again refused.

Back into Judge King's courtroom trooped the players. This time, however, there were two differences. The hunters, who had been only a shadowy presence in the background of the first proceeding, formally asked to join the case on the side of Hawaii in order to represent their interests. Second, Judge

*Humpback whale flukes (*Megaptera novaeangliae*), Southeast Alaska. By Frans Lanting/Minden Pictures.*

King refused this time to grant summary judgment. The state was claiming that the partial removal of feral sheep and goats had led to considerable regeneration of the forest, and he decided it should be given the opportunity to prove its contention that a small population of sheep could be kept in the area without harming the palila.

Unfortunately for the state's case, all the experts agreed that for the palila ever to have a chance of escaping from the endangered species list, all mouflon sheep, all feral sheep, and all feral goats would have to be eradicated. That was that. A small number of sheep might be able to coexist with a small number of palila, or they might not, owing to the painfully slow growth of the trees. As the scientists told the court, the only way to find out for sure just how far you could let the palila population decline without bringing on extinction would be to let it go extinct. Then you'd know.

This message came through loud and clear during the four days of trial held in the summer of 1986. Sherwood put a parade of scientists on the witness stand, all of whom said that the only way to give the palila a fighting chance to recover was to get rid of all the sheep and goats still on Mauna Kea. (When the trial got underway there were actually more feral sheep and goats on the mountain than there had been when the

court ordered their removal, a situation that did not amuse Judge King.)

There was a considerable sense of *déjà vu* during the second trial. The case was, after all, a virtual carbon copy of the first palila lawsuit, and most of the same people—lawyers, scientists, judge—had participated in the first case. The big difference was the intervention this time of the hunting clubs and hunters. This may explain why the state even bothered to resist the Legal Defense Fund's demand that the mouflon sheep be removed, since it was a legal long shot to try to convince Judge King that although the feral animals were bad for the palila, the wild sheep were not.

But the hunters' lobby in Hawaii is quite powerful. It had persuaded the state to fight the case, and the hunting clubs and individuals joined in to help. They needn't have bothered. After hearing the witnesses and oral arguments, Judge King took the case under advisement. Six months later he ruled, again in favor of the bird. A pro forma appeal was taken to the Ninth Circuit Court of Appeals, which again sustained Judge King. This time the state cooperated: even before the Ninth Circuit issued its opinion in early 1988, the state reported that all sheep and goats had been removed from the forest. The recovery of the palila had begun.

The Red-Cockaded Woodpecker

Before white settlers began managing the landscape for their own purposes, fires swept through the pine forests of the American Southeast every three to five years. Many forests in Florida burned every year. Red-cockaded woodpeckers, *picoides borealis,* depended on such periodic burns. It is no accident that the birds' range coincides with the part of the country most prone to lightning storms. The lightning started fires that kept undergrowth from clogging the understory of the woods but did not seriously harm living trees. Without fire, the understory grows until invaders—pileated woodpeckers and squirrels—that prefer a dense forest drive the red-cockadeds from their cavities. Fires maintained exactly the kind of forest the woodpeckers need for their nesting and feeding.

And not only woodpeckers benefitted from the burns, of course. The red-cockaded woodpecker, like the northern spotted owl that we shall examine presently, is called an indicator species because by measuring the relative vitality of its population an observer can draw fairly reliable conclusions about scores of other species that call the same habitat home. The particular set of circumstances that have put the red-cockaded woodpecker into this book have imperiled dozens of other species in its ecosystem.

Red-cockaded woodpeckers—the cockade is a dash of color just above and to the rear of the male bird's eye, seldom visible—are unusual in several respects. They are the only woodpeckers that build homes in living trees. This is no small accomplishment: it can take five years or more for an individual to peck out a cavity. Consequently, the birds tend to be extremely loyal to their homes. Groups of birds have been observed in the same area for decades. New cavities are excavated simply to replace cavities that must be abandoned when the trees die.

If a colony—a group of cavity trees—is destroyed, the birds can't simply pack up and move somewhere else as some other species can and do with ease. When cavity trees are destroyed—as many have been by logging—the birds simply disappear. They probably perish, but no one knows for certain.

The trees the woodpeckers favor are mature pines in the forest. They must be old enough to have lost their lower branches and acquired a blight called red heart fungus, which enters through the knotholes. The blight softens the heartwood and makes cavity-carving easier than it otherwise would be. This generally happens to southern pines only after they pass the age of about eighty years.

A cavity tree is not hard to recognize, owing to another clever trick the bird has evolved. All around the cavity opening, the woodpeckers pierce the bark and release a flow of sticky sap that rings the tree for a foot or so below the cavity. This is thought to help protect the birds from snakes, and may help them find their homes when they return at dusk from a hard day's foraging.

Each bird gets its own cavity. A colony has only one female, often accompanied by her mate and a few young males, who help incubate eggs, gather food for the young, dig new cavities, and defend their foraging turf from red-cockaded competition. Young are usually reared in the male's tree. Colonies tend to be found in clusters. This clustering is thought to facilitate the movement of young females away from their parents' colony, thus keeping the gene pool well stirred.

The feeding activity of the red-cockadeds is divided by sex, rather like supper in a Turkish village. The males forage in the top of the forest, the females closer to the ground. For some reason they do not share dining rooms, though they eat the same assortment of insects, which they dig out from beneath the bark of old trees. Neither males nor females will forage on the ground. Without fire or mechanical removal of the midstory hardwoods, the females get squeezed out of their foraging spots.

Two centuries ago, red-cockaded woodpeckers were common from the tip of Florida to New Jersey and west into Texas. Civilization has changed all that. The suppression of fire and the campaign to control the southern pine beetle to preserve commercially valuable timber have combined to put the red-cockaded woodpecker on the endangered species list.

The bird was listed in 1970, and a team was appointed to write a recovery plan. The going was difficult right from the start. The timber industry is important to the economy of the Southeast, and protecting and restoring the woodpecker and its habitat would certainly affect logging and displease industry. The original recovery team, appointed in 1975, had five members. Two were biologists and one was a forester, all with strong ties to the timber industry. These three believed that the bird should not be on the list at all. The other two were ornithologists, including team leader Dr. Jerome Jackson, who was and continues to be the scientist most knowledgeable about the bird. He fought stubbornly for four years until, in 1979, a badly compromised recovery plan was adopted.

The plan established a 200-foot buffer zone around all colonies, wherein only careful selective logging would be permitted. Around the buffer, another 200 acres would be managed for the birds' benefit, with trees allowed to reach 80 or 100 years in age before cutting (depending on species), and mechanical thinning or controlled burning of the understory carried out.

The Forest Service refused to change its management style to accommodate the plan. The timber industry began a long-running attempt to have the bird removed from the list, giving us yet another bureaucratic addition to the dictionary: "delist." Dr. Jackson, as principal author of the recovery plan and head of the recovery team, fought fiercely against attempts to delist the bird, and he prevailed. Indeed, the original recovery plan was inadequate to the task of protecting the woodpecker, and the plan was withdrawn in 1982. It was rewritten by a Forest Service biologist and adopted in 1985.

The Forest Service is at the center of this struggle because although it manages only five percent of the pine-forested lands in the Southeast, its lands contain more than two-thirds of the remaining red-cockaded woodpecker colonies. Cutting is so

Red-cockaded woodpecker (Picoides borealis). *By C. C. Lockwood/Animals Animals.*

rapid that the acreage of old-growth pines in the region—in both public and private ownership—declined by sixty percent in the forty years following World War II.

Timber harvesting has hurt the red-cockaded woodpecker, as has the suppression of fire. But the campaign to eradicate the southern pine beetle may provide the *coup de grâce*. The pine beetle bores into the bark of pine trees. When enough of them attack a tree they can kill it. Large infestations of beetles can kill large stands of trees just as large herds of mouflon sheep can eventually kill large sections of mamane—naio forests. But there's a big difference. Pine beetles are native to pine forests. They're as much a part of the ecosystem as red-cockaded woodpeckers; indeed, they form part of the woodpecker's diet. The beetles become a problem only after years of even-age management of the forest. That is, after a clearcut, the forest planted on the site is all the same species and the same age. This sort of forest is terribly vulnerable to various kinds of adversity, especially insects. In the 1970s and '80s, the pine plantations of the Southeast have been wracked by a plague of beetles that has killed millions of trees worth a great deal of money. Thus there is another key difference between this situation and the palila's: the mamane—naio forest is of no particular economic significance.

Careful and observant scientists like Dr. Jackson explained that the problem was with the management philosophy pursued by the Forest Service and private landowners alike. Clearcutting and monoculture were formulas for disaster. The way to control the plague—and to save the natural diversity of the forest—was to return to a reasonable facsimile of the natural forest: many different kinds of trees of many ages growing together. But this sort of forest will not provide the kind of instant profit a one-species tree farm will, at least not in the short term. (No tree farm has existed long enough to prove its long-term economic superiority to a natural forest, but that isn't generally factored into the equation.)

In any event, the strategy devised by the Forest Service to control the pine beetle infestation was to clearcut buffer zones around commercially valuable stands of pines, even when those buffers had to be put through dedicated wilderness areas. Some buffers were small. Others were very large. A clearcut in the Kitsatchie Hills Wilderness in Arkansas measured 3,200 acres, three times the size of Central Park. The entire wilderness area included just 8,700 acres.

By the early 1980s, it was clear that red-cockaded woodpecker populations were declining throughout the bird's range. It was already all but extinct in Oklahoma, Kentucky, and Tennessee. Its last foothold was in the national forests from Florida to Texas, but researchers could find not one population that was stable, let alone increasing. Still the Forest Service pursued its single-minded program of clearcutting, to control the pine beetle and to provide timber to sawmills and pulp mills.

Clearcutting makes life hard if not impossible for red-cockaded woodpeckers for several reasons. It removes the aging trees in which the birds might carve out new cavities once their existing cavity trees die. It means that the birds have to fly farther to forage, which is an important consideration for a species that spends so much time and so many calories pecking out new cavities. Winging across the clearcuts puts the birds at risk of predation by raptors. Finally, the big open areas are thought to serve as a barrier to the dispersion of young females into new colonies.

The National Wildlife Federation had forced the Forest Service to improve its management of woodpecker habitat in the early 1980s, but when the big flare-up of pine beetles began in east Texas in 1982, all bets were off. By 1985 the cutting in wilderness areas was so widespread that litigation seemed the only possible recourse. In June, Legal Defense Fund attorney Doug Honnold, a young law associate from central Illinois, filed suit against the Forest Service in the federal district court at Tyler, Texas, 100-odd miles north of Houston and about 60 miles from the Louisiana border.

Honnold asked Judge William Steger to block cutting in the five Texas wilderness areas, pending completion by the Forest Service of sufficiently detailed environmental studies to permit it to select the best control strategy. He told the judge that if the injunction were granted, he would demonstrate at trial that the cutting not only harmed the forest, it also was ineffective in stopping the spread of the beetles.

The Forest Service argued that it had studied the situation constantly and that the control strategy, while not perfect, was better than nothing. The judge refused to stop the cutting, saying that the damage inflicted by the cutting was less than the damage being inflicted by the beetles. He did grant some relief to the plaintiffs in the form of two orders. From then on, in the Texas wilderness areas, no more rampant cutting of hardwoods would be permitted (the Forest Service had been clearing all species of trees, despite the fact that the beetles attack only pines). Further, cutting uninfested trees would be allowed only to protect woodpecker colonies or to halt the spread of the beetle. This, of course, is what the Forest Service said it was doing, but evidence submitted to the judge indicated that the cutting had been much more vigorous than necessary. Judge Steger then suggested that the attorneys for both sides prepare to try the case on its merits the following fall.

The Legal Defense Fund's annual meeting of staff and trustees was held a few days after Judge Steger's ruling came down. Honnold told other staff members that he was thinking of rewriting his suit and filing it in the district court in Washington, D.C., where he thought it might receive a more sympathetic hearing. He planned to ask the court to enjoin logging in four wilderness areas in Arkansas, Louisiana, and Mississippi. The senior lawyers on the Legal Defense Fund staff were dubious, but Honnold was undeterred and refiled his case. It was assigned to Judge Gerhard Gesell.

On July 31, 1985, a scant six weeks after Judge Steger's ruling, Judge Gesell issued the injunction Honnold sought. All cutting in the four wilderness areas would be stopped unless it could be shown to be necessary to protect red-cockaded woodpeckers. Judge Gesell ordered the Forest Service to prepare site-specific environmental impact statements before going ahead with any logging in the four areas.

A complicating factor in developing a strategy for this case and many others was the National Forest Management Act of 1976. The enactment of that law followed a decision in a lawsuit brought by the Legal Defense Fund's Jim Moorman and others involving the Monongahela National Forest in West Virginia, where the court held that clearcutting violated the Forest Service's charter. The National Forest Management Act orders the Forest Service to adopt long-range management plans for all the national forests. The planning process provides for citizen participation and the right to appeal final plans, but it has proved a tool of ambiguous utility. The Forest Service has used it as a shield against judicial review. Frequently, the Forest Service will issue a final plan, environmental groups will appeal it to the office of the chief of the Forest Service, and there it will sit, sometimes for years. Meanwhile, the cutting continues. If the appellants try to go to court, lawyers from the Forest Service will argue that it is premature to ask a court to review the matter since the agency still hasn't ruled on the appeal.

Meanwhile, a debate ensued among the lawyers and conservationists interested in the Texas litigation. Honnold wanted to drop the case, sensing that to pursue it would be fruitless. His Texas counterpart, veteran lawyer Ned Fritz, who represented the Texas Committee on Natural Resources, wanted to push ahead. Eventually the decision was taken out of their hands: the case was transferred from Judge Steger to Judge Robert Parker.

Honnold did an about-face. The appearance of a new judge on the case gave him the opportunity to challenge the Forest Service strategy of hiding behind the forest-plan defense. If an urgent claim could be stressed—such as the imminent extinction of the red-cockaded woodpecker—then the judge might agree to review the forest plan itself.

Whereas the red-cockaded woodpecker had been kept in the background of the first two suits, it assumed center stage in these proceedings. This was because of a new survey conducted by Richard Conner, a biologist with the Forest Service, which confirmed that the red-cockaded woodpecker population on the Texas national forests was in rapid decline.

The trial, in February 1988, lasted four days. The government argued that Honnold was trying to resurrect matters that had already been dealt with by the court. They wrangled over the point when a forest plan was ripe for judicial review. But the red-cockaded woodpecker study was a key ingredient.

Witness after witness testified that clearcutting was wiping out the birds. When a specific instance of cutting too close to a colony was mentioned, the forest supervisor tried to argue that the birds must have moved in following the logging. Judge Parker wasn't buying. He found that the Forest Service was in violation of the Endangered Species Act and ordered it to stop even-age management within a 1,200-meter radius of all known colonies of red-cockaded woodpeckers. Altogether, this put about one-fourth of all the Texas national forest lands— 300,000 acres—off limits to most logging and forced a rewrite of the management plan for the forest. The Forest Service appealed the order and, as this book was being prepared for publication, the matter was still pending.

Judge Parker's order was unusual not only in that it effectively threw out a management plan that was not yet final and official, it also ruled illegal practices that were in fact in accordance with the Forest Service's duly adopted recovery plan for the birds.

Elated by the turn of events in Texas, Honnold and his colleagues Federico Cheever and Mark Hughes suggested to the Forest Service that it ought to apply Judge Parker's formula to all its red-cockaded woodpecker habitat in the Southeast. The Forest Service was unenthusiastic. The lawyers began sending letters announcing their intention to file suit against each of the sixteen national forests in the region, and the agency finally caved in. Under threat of suit, it announced it was putting more than a million acres of red-cockaded woodpecker habitat in the southeastern national forests off limits to clearcutting. For the birds, it finally looked as if there might be some hope.

Owl of the Ancient Forest

The northern spotted owl is the Pacific Northwest's biological equivalent of the red-cockaded woodpecker. Both birds are scarce and getting scarcer. Both have had their habitat decimated by logging over the past century. Both are thought to be reliable indicators of the overall health of their ecosystems. Both are fiercely controversial: admired by environmentalists and detested by the timber industry.

Apart from their biological differences, the most important difference between the two birds is a bureaucratic abstraction. The red-cockaded woodpecker is listed as an endangered species by the federal government. At the time this story began, the northern spotted owl was not. The reason was mainly political and economic: the timber industry didn't want the owl listed, and the industry is very powerful in the Pacific Northwest, even more powerful than it is in the South.

Like the woodpecker, the owl depends on old-growth forests, in this case the forests of Washington, Oregon, and northern California. It is part of the complex ecosystem that has evolved with these ancient forests, whose climax species are redwood, hemlock, and Douglas fir. Spotted owls are no more at home in post-clearcut monocultures than red-cockaded woodpeckers are. Logging in the Northwest has been just as vigorous as logging in the Southeast, maybe more so.

Of the estimated 17 million acres of old growth that once existed in Oregon and Washington, for example, only 3 or 4 million remain. Most of this is on federal lands: timber companies have had no compunction whatever in liquidating ancient trees on their own lands, and private owners are not bound by that pesky sustained-yield notion the Forest Service is supposed to abide by. By several accounts, all old growth in Oregon and Washington on private land was expected to be gone by 1990 or soon thereafter. Between a half-million and a million acres are preserved in four national parks and several

*Northern spotted owl (*Strix occidentalis*) in old-growth forest. By Pat & Tom
Leeson/Photo Researchers, Inc.*

national forest wildernesses. The rest—perhaps three million acres on lands managed by the Forest Service and the Bureau of Land Management—is what the fighting is all about. It is also where the future of the spotted owl, if it has one, lies.

One reason why you read qualifiers about how many acres of old growth remain in a certain area is that the very term is imprecise. The Forest Service, with its pronounced bias toward timber production, tends to go by a liberal definition of old growth, including younger trees than some biologists do, which leads it to a far higher estimate than environmental groups tend to use. In either event, the number is a great deal smaller than it once was, as is the number of spotted owls. Most estimates put the number of surviving northern spotted owls between 5,000 and 10,000, dangerously close to the point of no recovery.

And the owl, whose numbers are roughly the same as those of the red-cockaded woodpecker, did not have the dubious support of the endangered species program. Consequently, in the spring of 1987, Vic Sher, a young attorney in the Legal Defense Fund's brand-new Seattle office, submitted a petition to the Fish and Wildlife Service. It asked the agency to list the owl as endangered on the Olympic Peninsula and southwest Oregon and threatened everywhere else it is known to exist. Sher was ably assisted by Andy Stahl, a forester who had moved from the National Wildlife Federation's Portland office to join the new Legal Defense Fund operation. Stahl had been waging the old-growth fight for several years, and the chance to team up with an aggressive organization of lawyers was irresistible.

Stahl, for his part, was a gold mine for Sher and Todd True, the second attorney in the two-lawyer office. Stahl knew a great deal about the spotted owl, about the Forest Service, about forestry. Best of all, he knew nearly all the people in the region concerned with the issues. He helped coordinate with the more than twenty organizations that joined in the petition.

When Fish and Wildlife denied the petition—under circumstances the General Accounting Office later reported to have been contrary to established policy—Sher filed a lawsuit aimed at forcing the service to list the owl pursuant to the Endangered Species Act. Following much searching of souls, all the appropriate groups in the Northwest joined as plaintiffs.

The reasons for their hesitation were grounded in public relations. Logging is widely perceived as vital to the region's economy, and some environmentalists feared losing the support of citizens and politicians who might find the spotted-owl stance too radical.

Another brake on all-out litigation under the Endangered Species Act is the lesson learned from the lawsuit concerning a small fish native to the Little Tennessee River. It was called the snail darter, and it wasn't even discovered until a big dam being built by the Tennessee Valley Authority was half complete. Litigation halted construction of the dam for many months, a series of court decisions sustained all the way to the United States Supreme Court. Eventually Congress exempted the project from the Endangered Species Act, and the dam was completed, snail darter be damned.

As this drama played out, editorialists, cartoonists, and pundits of many hues derided any and all who stood up for the snail darter. They heaped ridicule and scorn on anyone who would put insignificant animals in the way of capital-P progress. The experience made many people very uncomfortable, and it has reined in the ardor of some who might have vigorously defended other humble creatures.

The key reason for caution on the part of organizations that might instinctively side with the spotted owl—or the grizzly or some other highly visible rare creature—was a fear that if litigation were successful it might provoke a powerful backlash that would lead to crippling amendments to the Endangered Species Act, or sweep away the law altogether. This has not happened to date, but various senators and representatives, mainly from the interior regions of the country, have mounted worrisome threats and delayed reauthorization of the act on several occasions. However, people like Rick Sutherland, the executive director of the Legal Defense Fund, are inclined to scoff at such concern about losing this or any other law through a backlash. "A law that is not enforced is worse than no law at all," he insists.

In any event, the bullet was bitten and the suit brought. It was, as far as the Legal Defense Fund's lawyers could make out, only the second time anyone had filed such a case. (The first, also by a Legal Defense Fund lawyer, involved a subspecies of king salmon that spawns in California's Sacramento River.) It is very difficult to persuade a court to overrule an agency on matters involving scientific judgment.

That's what made the spotted owl case so attractive. Sher, True, and Stahl knew almost all the scientists who were studying the owls, and there seemed to be an impregnable consensus that the birds were in terrible shape and ought to be listed. If ever one could prove that a Fish and Wildlife Service decision were indefensible, this ought to be the time.

The case was timely in part because of a change in Endangered Species Act regulations adopted in 1982. While one functionary was trying to gut the definition of "harm" under those regulations, as reported earlier in this chapter, someone else was cinching up a dangerous loophole that might allow a plea of economic distress to override biological imperatives. Following 1982 it was the law that the Fish and Wildlife Service had to rely solely on biological information in deciding whether or not to list a creature.

In the case of the spotted owl, it was palpably true that the agency had succumbed to the economic entreaties of mill owners, timber barons, and forest-belt politicians. Proving it to a federal judge was something else again. Until, that is, Beth Stout of the National Wildlife Federation quietly attended a speech by David Riley of the Fish and Wildlife Service. Riley was speaking to members of the Izaak Walton League, most of whom he obviously thought were unhappy with the agency's decision against listing the bird. He spoke of the frightening backlog of species that were then candidates for listing (5,546) and of the difficulty of assembling data from the scores of

Killer whales (Orcinus orca), *Washington coast. By F. Gohier/Photo Researchers, Inc.*

scientists studying the owls. Then he said that a decision to list the species would be "very detrimental to the whole region. Now that's not a reason not to list," he went on, "but certainly it weighed heavily on our mind. . . ." To the lawyers, this seemed a clear admission that economic factors had played a role in determining the decision, which is illegal.

The heart of the case, though, was whether the bird is endangered or threatened biologically. To justify its refusal to list the bird, the Fish and Wildlife Service cited the work of Mark Boyce of the University of Wyoming, who said that the data did not show positively that the bird was in peril of extinction. Boyce was the only scientist studying the spotted owl who felt that way, but one was enough for the Fish and Wildlife Service. It might be good enough for the court.

Andy Stahl got on the phone to Boyce and asked him about his studies and those of his colleagues. He then told Boyce how the Service had paraphrased his work in court papers. Boyce said he was being misquoted. He wrote a letter to the Fish and Wildlife Service, saying he was very displeased by the misuse of his study. With that, the agency's case dissolved.

Judge Thomas Zilly called a hearing for late 1988 and patiently listened to the arguments from both sides. Then he issued his ruling, on the spot, from the bench. He found the Fish and Wildlife Service in violation of the law for failing to give a plau-

sible reason for not listing the spotted owl. He gave the agency ninety days to come up with a new decision, a new justification of its decision, or both.

Meanwhile, Sher, True, and law associate Corrie Yackulic were fighting on many other fronts in defense of the spotted owl and old-growth forests. They forced the Forest Service to undertake new studies when defaulted timber sales were offered for resale. They held up old-growth sales in western Oregon on lands managed by the Bureau of Land Management. They blocked sales on Forest Service lands in Oregon and Washington. At one stage, in the spring of 1989, virtually all new sales of old-growth timber on federal land in Oregon and Washington were suspended owing to Legal Defense Fund litigation.

In late April word leaked out that the Fish and Wildlife Service had decided to recommend that the owl be listed as threatened throughout its range. The news made front pages throughout much of the country. Environmentalists were jubilant and at the same time wary of possible reaction in Congress. The timber industry howled that the decision would bring economic ruin to the region. Knowledgeable observers, including notably a former regional officer of the Fish and Wildlife Service, said that the industry's fears were much exaggerated. Late in the summer of 1989 some legislators from the Northwest were trying to persuade Congress to limit drastically litigation over old-growth timber sales, an attempt to solve the problem by ignoring it. The struggle, like most battles over declining resources, will continue.

In the late 1980s the battle over old-growth forests—the term "ancient forests" seemed to be coming into vogue—dominated environmental affairs in the conifer belt. Initiatives were mounted to halt the export of logs to Japan, in part to protect millworkers' jobs. The economies of Oregon and Washington were being remodeled to depend more heavily on tourism and second-growth forests. There seemed to be a chance to preserve a considerable fraction of the remaining old growth in its primeval state. Whether that happens will depend on a myriad of interrelated factors, many political. As the fight entered its critical stages, it was clear that the litigation improved environmentalists' hand.

"Harm" on the High Seas

Some years ago, a particularly fiendish kind of fishing gear was invented: the drift gillnet, so called because it drifts with the rolls and swells of the ocean and catches fish by the gills. Most drift gillnets are made of plastic filament that is nearly invisible. They hang straight down in the water, a lethal curtain kept aloft by floats and taut by weights. They are twenty-five feet deep—or more, depending on what the fishermen are after—and as much as thirty miles long. At any given moment, tens of thousands of miles of these nets are deployed throughout the Earth's oceans.

They are an equal opportunity destroyer. No matter whether the intended victim is salmon, squid, billfish, pomfret, albacore, or another species, the driftnet does not discriminate. It will catch and frequently drown almost anything unfortunate enough to happen by and too big to pass through the mesh: porpoises, seals, sea lions, dolphins, an occasional killer whale, and scores of species of seabirds. And despite all the havoc, they are inefficient: studies suggest that more than one fourth of the sought-after fish that are caught in drift gillnets die, slip free from the nets, and sink to the bottom: a dead waste.

This nightmare is going on all over the world and with particular intensity in the northern Pacific Ocean, a rich fishing ground where ships from Japan, Taiwan, and South Korea catch thousands of tons of seafood—mainly salmon and squid—every year. The cost of those fish in terms of what's called the "incidental" catch of marine mammals and seabirds is almost unbelievable.

The exact figures are unknown and difficult to estimate, since records kept by fishing operations in international waters are sketchy, suspect, or simply unavailable. Extrapolating from data gathered in United States waters in the northern Pacific and the Bering Sea, however, it is clear that tens of thousands of marine mammals and hundreds of thousands of seabirds perish as unintended victims of these fisheries each year. Add to this the hundreds of thousands of porpoises still being killed in the international tuna fleet's purse-seines, and the carnage in the Pacific is immense.

What, one might ask, is the United States, with its proud tradition of protecting marine mammals, doing about all this slaughter? The answer is: more than most other countries, but far from enough. The reason is that this country is caught in a difficult bind, trying to protect marine mammals and its own commercial and subsistence fishermen on the one hand and trying to maintain good relations with its important Pacific trading partners on the other. This has led to a trade-off where marine mammals are too often the losers.

Under the Marine Mammal Protection Act all marine mammals are protected, which is essentially the same as if they all were listed as endangered on the Fish and Wildlife Service's list. The government can allow the killing of marine mammals—of any species whatever—only if the Secretary of Commerce can issue a formal scientific finding that such killing won't do the species serious damage.

It is well documented that the incidental take of marine mammals in the northern Pacific includes Dall's porpoises, northern fur seals, sea lions, harbor porpoises, Pacific white-sided dolphins, northern right whale dolphins, and killer whales. Yet when the National Marine Fisheries Service issued a fishing permit to the Japanese fleet in the spring of 1987, it sanctioned the taking only of Dall's porpoise, the reason being that Dall's porpoise was the only species for which data were reliable enough to support a finding of no serious harm. Because the northern fur seal population, by contrast, has declined alarmingly in recent years, the administrator of NMFS said that the taking of fur seals was in no way condoned by the permit, was still illegal, and would be punished by fines. Yet he knew for certain that the Japanese driftnets would entangle fur seals. In effect, he issued a permit for one species (porpoises) that would surely result in the taking of another species (fur seals). Even the pledge to impose penalties for other takings was a none-too-reassuring promise, given that NMFS had seldom prosecuted parties guilty of illegal takings in the past.

The Legal Defense Fund's Lauri Adams, from Oregon and Harvard Law School, filed suit against NMFS for issuing an illegal permit. Though Adams's office is in Juneau, she filed the suit in Washington, D.C., since the defendant was a federal agency and since she could get help from two staff lawyers there, Howard Fox and Robert Dreher. They asked the court to suspend the permit, the sooner the better.

The fishery has a very short season, however, about six weeks in early summer. By the time all the briefs were complete and a hearing could be held, the boats were already underway to the fishing ground.

Judge Joyce Green seemed sympathetic to the marine mammals' cause, but at the same time cautious. She ruled that the permit was illegal but she wouldn't stop the fishing. If her ruling held up on appeal, however, the fishery would not be permitted to operate the following year.

An appeal was duly filed; by a vote of two to one Judge Green's opinion was sustained. This was the spring of 1988 and the fishermen were getting worried. Might they really lose their permits to fish for salmon in that part of the ocean? They

Northern fur seals (Callorhinus ursinus), Pribilof Islands, Alaska. By Yogi Kaufman/Peter Arnold, Inc.

asked the Supreme Court to let them fish while they readied formal papers seeking review of the decision in the high court. Chief Justice Rehnquist threw the decision to the full court, which refused to issue a stay. The fishing boats could stay home.

Meanwhile, Congress was revising the Marine Mammal Protection Act. When it finally passed a revised act in late 1988, the question of incidental taking was resolved thusly: incidental catches of marine mammals could be permitted for American fishermen, but not others, for a period of five years. The lag was meant to provide time for the development of new fishing methods that will protect the birds and mammals.

The new provisions were clearly aimed at the North Pacific salmon fishery, and when the Japanese fishermen asked the Supreme Court to review the Appeals Court decision itself—the request referred to above was simply to stay it pending this requested review—the high court again refused. Litigation had

spared no one knows exactly how many fur seals, Dall's porpoises, and countless other mammals and birds.

The race to stop the extinction of thousands upon thousands of species across the world goes on. The rate of loss is accelerating, principally owing to the rapid decimation of the world's tropical rainforests. As American environmentalists turn their attention to this and other international environmental problems and controversies, there's no doubt that legal minds and legal strategies will be called on to help. As the last decade of the twentieth century begins, the Sierra Club Legal Defense Fund is seeking ways to become active in international legal issues, not only to protect endangered species but also to help stem global warming, pollution of the oceans, and destruction of the rainforests.

Sea lions, seals, and plovers, California coast. By Frans Lanting/Minden Pictures.

CHAPTER SIX

The Northern Rockies
Paper Transactions and Grizzly Bears

I
t might have been better if Henry Ford had been interested in botany, say, or grand opera, or curing the common cold. But no, he turned his considerable genius toward contriving an automobile for Everyman. His brainchild has had a more profound effect on civilization and the environment than any other single invention.

In order to build, fuel, and drive our massive fleet of cars and trucks, we have splashed asphalt and concrete across the land, punched holes into valleys and riverbeds and mountains in search of oil, colonized foreign lands to acquire rubber and more petroleum, rewritten laws on liability, pollution, and nuisance, and generally shaped our economy and our entire way of life around the internal-combustion engine. With the crude oil often came natural gas, a marvelously convenient, clean-burning fuel that was soon flickering beneath furnaces and water heaters in homes and boiling water in thermal powerplants. Together, oil and natural gas would become seemingly indispensable.

At the beginning of the 1980s it was conservatively estimated that one of six jobs in the American economy was related in one way or another to the

Grizzly sow and cubs (Ursus arctos)*, northern Rocky Mountains. By Pat & Tom Leeson/ Photo Researchers, Inc.*

automobile. The very thirsty and demanding automobile. Twice in the decade of the 1970s, the Organization of Petroleum Exporting Countries, a cartel made up of most (but by no means all) of the Third World's crude oil producers, shook the economies of the West to their foundations. The OPEC producers throttled back on their production, gasoline prices went through the ceiling, and American motorists fumed as they sat in long lines waiting to fill the gas tanks of their cars.

In the medium term, these supply curtailments had at least two effects. One was belatedly to produce a sharp increase in consumer demand for smaller, more efficient cars, and the second was to spark renewed interest in exploration for and production of domestic oil (and natural gas), which had been undersold by the OPEC producers for years.

The first result was welcomed by most people, particularly by conservationists, who had quietly cheered on the OPEC activities as likely to raise the price of gasoline and other fuels and thereby suppress demand. The other consequence of rising prices, though, was a push to go after marginal deposits of hydrocarbons that until then had been too difficult and expensive to extract to be worth the producers' while. As the price of crude oil soared past ten, twenty, thirty dollars a barrel, petroleum geologists sketched plans to search for oil in all kinds of out-of-the-way places.

A principal destination was the wild mountain country along the spine of the Rocky Mountains, from Grand Teton National Park north, past Yellowstone, and up to Glacier National Park on the border with Canada. This is the last redoubt of the mighty grizzly bear in the contiguous United States.

The grizzly holds a very special place in the American mind, for a variety of reasons. He is the biggest, fiercest, most ornery beast white men and Indians have shared their living space with, and one of the fastest. He is also, physically speaking, closer in build to man than any creature except the primates, and we don't have any of those. He is as disdainful and unfearful of his fellow creatures as man is, and, some will even argue, he can think.

For all that, the grizzly is rather shy except under certain circumstances. One of those circumstances involves running out of living space or being presented free handouts or garbage-dump snacks like penned-up cattle or sheep. As soon as white settlers began to tame the West, they inevitably came into conflict with the bears.

Once, the bones tell us, there were as many as 100,000 grizzlies scattered from Canada to Mexico, from the plains to the Pacific shore, ten thousand in California alone. They eat almost anything, dead or alive, from meat to fish and berries to roots. They had no adversaries apart from the weather and

South fork of the Sun River, Bob Marshall Wilderness, Montana.

Dwarf fireweed and paintbrush, Deep Creek, Lewis and Clark National Forest, Montana.

old age until white settlers showed up with repeating rifles. As William H. Wright wrote in 1909, "The first chapter of the history of the grizzly is the beginning of the story's end. When my grandfather was born, the grizzly had never been heard of. If my grandson ever sees one, it will likely be in the bear pit of a zoological garden."

It hasn't come to that yet, just ninety-nine percent of the way. The state flag of California bears a likeness of a grizzly; the last wild grizzly in that state was killed in the 1920s. The great brown bears of the Lower Forty-eight now mostly live in the northern Rockies. Their total population is unknown, but certainly well below one thousand. Their only hope for survival is to be left alone, but unfortunately for the bears, their last homes harbor valuable timber and may overlie significant deposits of hydrocarbons.

Much of the northern Rockies lies above a geological formation that sounds like a girdle for beer guzzlers: the Overthrust Belt. Rather than a cosmetic device, however, it is the region where one tectonic plate rides up over another. When plates collide this way, the topography is nearly always spectacular, as it is here. Such geology often means earthquakes. Sometimes it means volcanos or other geothermal activities, as at Yellowstone. And sometimes it indicates deposits of oil and gas. Estimates of the petroleum hidden in pockets deep within the Overthrust Belt range all the way to fifteen billion barrels (the North Slope of Alaska is thought to contain perhaps ten billion, not counting whatever may or may not be found beneath the Arctic National Wildlife Refuge). Most estimates are more modest; there's a fair chance that very little oil and gas worth extracting lies there. Finding out for sure—and finding out in a way that doesn't wreck other resources atop any petroleum deposits—is what the present story is all about.

In one sense, this tale begins in 1964, with passage of the Wilderness Act. That law was the culmination of fourteen years' work by wilderness advocates from around the country, led by Howard Zahniser of The Wilderness Society and David Brower of the Sierra Club. The law established the National Wilderness Preservation System and outlined a framework that Congress and federal land management agencies could follow to set wild and beautiful lands aside, forever preserved from logging, roads, cabins or other buildings, dams, tennis courts— almost all human contrivances.

The 1964 act incorporated several existing wildernesses in the new system and ordered the Forest Service, the National Park Service, the Fish and Wildlife Service, and other agencies to review their lands and recommend to Congress other areas that should be considered for designation as wilderness.

All prohibitions on development in existing wilderness and wilderness candidate areas were absolute, with one giant exception. Protection from mining and oil and gas exploration and development was deferred for twenty years. It was the price conservationists had to pay to get a wilderness act at all. Western mining interests insisted that wildernesses be left open to mineral exploration and exploitation until 1984. Thus, as signed into law by Lyndon Johnson in the fall of 1964, the Wilderness Act left wilderness areas open to mineral entry until midnight on December 31, 1983.

But a funny thing happened on the way to 1984. Though several hundred applications were made for oil and gas leases in wilderness areas and potential wilderness areas, only seventeen were approved. Most were filed and not acted on.

There is an important difference between the way the government deals with oil, coal, and natural gas on the one hand and "hardrock" minerals on the other. Under the Mining Law of 1872, public lands that are not "withdrawn" are open for exploration. If a prospector discovers valuable mineral deposits, he has the right to develop them. The government in that instance retains some control over the miner's activities on the surface, although through another procedure known as patenting a prospector can gain ownership of the surface *and* the minerals beneath.

For oil, coal, and natural gas the system is different, though it wasn't always so. Originally, oil and gas were claimed and owned in the same manner as hardrock minerals. But a panic in the early part of the century—when the government feared that the country was about to run out of petroleum—led to the enactment of the Mineral Leasing Act of 1920, which provides that public lands "may" be leased by the Secretary of the Interior. The secretary issues the leases through the Bureau of Land Management, even if the surface is managed by an agency of another department, such as the Forest Service within the Agriculture Department. There are no claims or patents, but rather leases that the government sells, either at auction or simply to the first person or company that offers to buy. (A scandal-ridden lottery system was abolished by Congress in the late 1980s.) Leases are frequently sold before anyone knows whether there are any hydrocarbons worth extracting under the land in question. The public lands are perforated with dry holes that industry has leased for very little money.

Just how much attention will be paid to environmental considerations before the issuance of any leases has concerned environmentalists for the past several decades.

By the mid-1970s, the oil and gas industry was fed up with the delays in getting leases approved. For more than a decade it had asked the Forest Service for permission to explore for deposits in various wilderness areas and in areas that the agency was reviewing for possible addition to the wilderness system. The Forest Service had accepted the lease applications, put them in a file cabinet, and ignored them. The applications weren't refused, they simply weren't acted upon. The Forest Service may have wanted to reject the applications but feared it might provoke a fight it couldn't win. In the 1950s some lease applications were rejected on environmental grounds. The petroleum industry sued and tried to persuade the courts that "the Secretary *may*" lease really means "the Secretary *must*" lease, but the industry lost. Why the Forest Service got timid in the '70s is a detail that remains to be revealed.

For a long time, in fact, it didn't matter, since the oil and gas companies had more leases than they could handle. But when OPEC got into the act, not only did the price of oil and

*Fall-colored aspens, Tie Canyon,
The Palisades, Targhee National
Forest, Idaho.*

gas climb sharply, there was also a strong push to identify and explore all possible domestic stocks of hydrocarbons.

The organization that first filed suit in a long series of post-OPEC cases was an inadvertent product of the successes of the nonprofit environmental law movement. Industry could see all too readily the successes environmental lawyers had enjoyed during the 1970s. It decided to establish nonprofit law firms of its own. Contributions would be deductible from taxes and the aura of a nonprofit halo might curry some public sympathy. Thus were born in California the Pacific Legal Foundation and in Colorado the Mountain States Legal Foundation. These organizations would file cases either in their own names, or on behalf of commercial clients, or both. They put a new spin on the phrase "public interest," which they vociferously claimed to represent.

In the late 1970s, Mountain States, led by a lawyer from Wyoming named James Watt, filed suit against the Interior and Agriculture secretaries to force an end to the practice of sitting on lease applications in the national forests. The case was heard by Judge Clarence Brimmer in the federal court in Wyoming. Judge Brimmer agreed with Mountain States that the government wasn't playing fair. He gave the government three options: grant the lease applications, deny the applications and have a good reason for doing so, or ask Congress to pass a law that would withdraw the areas in question from leasing. The government did not appeal Judge Brimmer's decision.

Next, a trade group called the Rocky Mountain Oil and Gas Association filed suit in the federal district court, also in Wyoming, against the Bureau of Land Management, seeking a similar order to govern BLM lands being reviewed for their wilderness potential. This time, though, the facts were significantly different. The agency was rejecting lease applications in potential wilderness areas based on a legal opinion by the Solicitor of the Interior Department. He cited specific provisions in the Federal Land Policy and Management Act that required BLM to keep wild areas wild until Congress had time to decide whether to keep them so forever.

Legal Defense Fund attorney Laurens Silver represented four national environmental groups and intervened on the side of the government. The Oil and Gas Association, however, found another sympathetic Wyoming judge in the person of Ewing Kerr, who referred to the environmental organizations that intervened in the case as "special interest groups."

This brings up a little-understood aspect of most environmental lawsuits: they are intensely political. That is to say, their outcome depends to a great degree on the political views of the judge who happens to hear the case. The oil and gas cases under discussion are a good example. Judicial opinions that begin with a description of the natural beauty of the mountains, valleys, streams, and animals invariably end with a pro-environment decision. Opinions that ruminate extensively on the energy crisis and the country's need for secure supplies of oil and gas inevitably go the other way. Judge Kerr's opinion was of the latter variety and he granted summary judgment for the plaintiffs.

The intervenors and the government appealed the decision to the Tenth Circuit Court of Appeals. That court reversed Judge Kerr and said that the BLM was acting in accordance with law and the will of Congress. It was a very important affirmation of government's power to lease only under conditions that protected potential wilderness areas.

Nevertheless, the informal grace period for wilderness areas and potential wilderness areas—particularly in the national forests—seemed to be at an end. The Forest Service recommended the blanket issuance of leases covering the entire Palisades area, a quarter-million-acre roadless area in the Bridger-Teton and Targhee National Forests, south of Yellowstone on the Wyoming-Idaho border.

The recommendation to lease was based on a cursory environmental assessment. That assessment came to the conclusion that simply issuing a lease had no significant environmental impact—had no impact on the environment at all, in fact—and that therefore no environmental impact statement was necessary. The Sierra Club Legal Defense Fund, represented by staff attorney Karin Sheldon, filed suit to force preparation of an impact statement, and the battle was joined.

It was a battle over timing, played out over a decade and through many lawsuits. The government, and the oil and gas companies with it, argued that signing a lease was a simple "paper transaction" that harmed not one grizzly bear, pine tree, or tadpole. When and if oil or gas was found, they argued, that would be the time to do the environmental studies.

Sheldon and her colleagues riposted that issuing the lease was the point of no return. It vests rights in the leaseholder that virtually guarantee the right to develop the lease. Once a lease is issued, the government would be powerless to stop extraction of oil or gas no matter how environmentally damaging it might prove to be. The time for the environmental studies was before any promises are made, they insisted.

The industry grumped that most wells turn up dry or without enough oil or gas to be worth extracting. Environmental studies are expensive. The environmentalists countered that if industry insisted on the absolute right to exploit its leases, it had to be willing to measure potential environmental harm before the commitment was irreversible.

The Palisades case was filed in the U.S. District Court in Washington, D.C., and heard by Judge Aubrey Robinson. Judge Robinson ruled that no environmental impact statement was necessary because the leases contained provisions that left control over surface activities with the Forest Service.

The leases covered 247,000 acres of the Palisades, but only 28,000 could actually be "occupied." That is, all drilling rigs and other equipment would be confined to these 28,000 acres of islands dotted throughout the area. Oil and gas would be extracted from beneath the balance of the Palisades by drilling on a slant, at least in theory.

Sheldon did not contest the no-surface-occupancy areas, though she did worry about places where surface occupancy would be permitted, and where the Forest Service had put no limits on surface-disturbing activities. She appealed Judge

Marsh-marigolds, Hasley Basin, Maroon Bells/Snowmass Wilderness, Colorado.

Mountain ash and aspen trunks, The Palisades, Targhee National Forest, Idaho.

Robinson's ruling to the Court of Appeals for the District of Columbia. Her panel included judges George MacKinnon, Skelly Wright, and Supreme Court Justice-to-be Antonin Scalia.

Sheldon remembers that argument as a highlight of her legal career. She recalls entering the courtroom and standing before the bench to begin her argument. Judge Scalia almost immediately asked her a question she had not anticipated, a novel interpretation of the district court opinion. Her stomach descended to her shoetops. "My field of vision narrowed so that the audience disappeared, the other lawyers disappeared, even the other judges disappeared. It was just Judge Scalia and me," she says. "He was intensely interested in the case, and he questioned me for nearly an hour. It was exhilarating."

It was also successful. The panel unanimously reversed Judge Robinson and told the Forest Service it would have to conduct environmental impact studies if it wanted to issue leases without no-surface-occupancy stipulations.

James Watt, the lawyer from Mountain States Legal Foundation, had by this time been appointed Secretary of the Interior, over the vociferous protests of most of the major environmental organizations in the country. Watt's reputation as a sharp-tongued, ideologically rigid, development-minded advocate was proving to be, if anything, understated. He dismissed all who disagreed with him as extremists and questioned their patriotism. He divided people into two categories: liberals and Americans.

One of his early acts was to order a drastic switch in resource policies on federal lands. Development was the watchword. All the public lands, both onshore and off the coasts, should be explored for their possible mineral riches, Mr. Watt said. Some should actually be sold to private corporations or individuals. Others should be turned over to the states. ("Sagebrush rebels," as adherents of this view called themselves, were fond of demanding that the federal lands in the West be "returned" to the states, even though they had always been federal lands and had never belonged to the states.)

Watt claimed that he was in favor of "orderly" development now so as to preclude helter-skelter development later when civilization would begin running out of vital resources. His critics called him a front man for selfish commercial interests and demanded that he be replaced.

Whatever the motives, Watt's initiatives were bold. Within weeks of taking over the Interior Department, Watt announced that he was going to issue mineral leases in some of the most popular wilderness areas in the country—congressionally established wilderness areas, not just roadless areas being considered for wilderness. His list included the Maroon Bells in Colorado, the Alpine Lakes in Washington, the Capitan Mountains in New Mexico, and the Bob Marshall in Montana, one of the oldest and largest wilderness areas in the country.

The "Bob" was established in 1940, a million-and-a-half-acre paradise of granite peaks, glaciated valleys, trout-rich streams, and grizzly bears, elk, moose, wolves, and many other creatures. It lies next to two other wildernesses—the Scapegoat and the Great Bear. With other unprotected but wild country in all directions, the Bob is one of two places in the United States outside Alaska where it is still possible to get ten miles away from the nearest road. The other is in California, east of Mineral King.

Jim Watt's judgment was always suspect. He seemed to pick his fights with an eye toward mobilizing his opposition. In his wilderness-leasing ploy, he not only infuriated environmentalists and the public, he also ran afoul of his natural constituency: the congressional delegations from the West. No sooner had Watt announced the leasing plan than the House Interior Committee ordered him to withdraw the Bob, the Scapegoat, and the Great Bear from mineral leasing on an emergency basis, to last until 1984. Watt signed the withdrawal order but said publicly that he was doing so only under duress. He further said that he thought the House committee's order was illegal and tacitly invited someone to sue him.

Mountain States Legal Foundation and Pacific Legal Foundation were happy to oblige, in a case that became known as Watt versus Watt. Watt the Secretary refused to defend his own withdrawal order, and he leaned on the Justice Department to stay out of the case as well. The House and Senate committees therefore assigned their own lawyers to the case; they teamed up with Karin Sheldon and her colleague Bill Curtiss to defend the Interior Committee's right to order an emergency withdrawal.

Mountain States represented the interests of people who had filed more than 340 lease applications on the three wildernesses and were still awaiting word from the government. Their main argument was that Congress did not have the right to delegate to a committee of just one house the power to order a withdrawal of land. That, they argued, was usurping the constitutional power of the executive.

In the course of examining correspondence and other documents in the Interior Department's files, a process known politely as discovery, Curtiss and Sheldon came across letters from Pacific Legal Foundation's Ronald A. Zumbrum to William Coldiron, Interior's Solicitor, who was nominally defending Secretary Watt. Zumbrum asked for help, offered suggestions on strategy, complained of botched opportunities—all most irregular in light of the fact that Zumbrum and Coldiron were supposedly adversaries in the case. Coldiron never answered in writing and finally got word to Zumbrum that such behavior might backfire. It did. Curtiss and Sheldon gleefully provided copies of the Zumbrum letters to the press, which found all kinds of unsavory collusion indicated.

The hearing, held in the federal courthouse in Great Falls, Montana, in September 1981, was something of a circus. There were lawyers from Pacific Legal Foundation, from Mountain States Legal Foundation, from the Justice Department, and from the Sierra Club Legal Defense Fund. There were lawyers representing Montana Senator John Melcher and House Interior Committee members Morris Udall and Manuel Lujan.

The Justice Department lodged a feeble challenge to the plaintiffs' standing. When that motion was overruled by the judge, Justice immediately switched sides and agreed that the

Summer grasses, with the Scapegoat Wilderness in the distance, Lolo and Helena National Forest, Montana.

Deep Creek and the Sawtooth Range, Lewis and Clark National Forest, Montana.

*Bald eagles (*Haliaeetus leucocephalus*),
northern Montana. By Dan Suzio/
Animals Animals.*

one-house veto provision of the law under which the Interior Committee had ordered the withdrawal—the Federal Land Policy and Management Act—was unconstitutional.

Judge William J. Jameson drew the case. After hearing extensive argument, and based on an opinion just recently issued by the Supreme Court on the matter of one-house vetoes, he ruled in favor of the plaintiffs that the withdrawal the House had ordered Watt to make was unconstitutional and must be rescinded. But it was too late, much too late. Because of the publicity surrounding the case, the House simply found another tactic: it told Secretary Watt that he must not spend any money preparing for lease sales in designated wilderness and wilderness candidate areas. Again, the environmentalists had lost a lawsuit, but the bigger victory was achieved.

Watt then got too clever by half. He announced, in what appeared to be an off-the-cuff remark on "Meet the Press" one Sunday, that he would ask Congress to put all wilderness off limits to mineral leasing immediately, a ban that would run until the year 2000. Conservationists and legislators alike were taken off guard. Their public reactions were guarded and equivocal. Soon, though, they remembered that wilderness would be off limits to mineral leasing starting on January 1, 1984, and that that moratorium would last forever. Watt's deceptive suggestion was ignored. Mineral leasing in congressionally established wilderness areas was a dead letter.

❧

Leasing in de facto wilderness was quite another story. Just east of the Bob Marshall, on the sheer scarp of the Northern Rockies known as the Front Range, lie a series of parallel valleys running north to south that are bisected by a stream known as Deep Creek. The Deep Creek region, like the three wilderness areas it abuts on the west, is rich in many species of wildlife, including the threatened grizzly bear and the endangered grey wolf, bald eagle, and peregrine falcon.

When the Forest Service surveyed its holdings for potential new wildernesses, it had a report card. Areas could score points for beauty, for size, for remoteness, for wildlife. A perfect score was twenty-eight. Deep Creek scored twenty-eight. Nevertheless in early 1981 the Bureau of Land Management, part of the Watt Interior Department, issued nineteen oil and gas leases, covering 42,000 acres of Deep Creek. Again, as at Palisades, the Forest Service prepared only the sketchiest of environmental assessments, saying that a full environmental impact statement could wait until later.

After an unsuccessful administrative appeal, Legal Defense Fund attorney Stephan Volker filed suit, claiming violations of the National Environmental Policy Act and the Endangered Species Act. The industry argument in many of these cases is that they are merely asking initial permission to explore for oil and gas. For full-field development, they insist, there would be mitigation measures and extra environment-protecting precautions. As Steve Volker found, however, the exploration was every bit as critical as the eventual extraction.

As is the case throughout most of the Overthrust Belt, any oil and gas to be found at Deep Creek is at least 10,000 feet down. This means heavy-duty drilling equipment, which means roads: the equipment is too heavy to be lifted by helicopters. Each of the drill sites would cover as much territory as two football fields, with drill pads, pits for storing the highly toxic drilling mud, piles of pipe, generators, barracks, and an

Castle Reef, the Front Range, Lewis and Clark National Forest, Montana.

Elk cow (Cervus elaphus) *with weed seeds in fur, Montana. By Harry Engels/Animals Animals.*

office. Exploratory drilling is expensive, so companies like to keep the work going twenty-four hours a day, seven days a week. It's also noisy. The Forest Service conceded that at least fifteen such exploratory drilling operations would be built.

In addition to other concerns, Volker learned there had never been decent surveys of eagle nesting sites or of falcon nesting sites. There had been scant work done on wolves, grizzlies, or the Sun River elk herd, the biggest in that country.

Volker took his time, requesting masses of documents from agencies and scientists in a variety of locations. The discovery process took two years. He found evidence that the Interior Department knew full well that the site could not be restored to a pre-drilling condition for at least twenty years. The exploration, the government admitted, would plunge Deep Creek's perfect twenty-eight wilderness rating to a mediocre nineteen. The unofficial hope of the plaintiffs, led by the Bob Marshall Alliance, was to hold off the drillers until James Watt might be replaced by a more sympathetic Interior Secretary.

The hearing took place in the federal district court in Great Falls, Montana, in early 1984. Volker's case was assigned to Judge Paul Hatfield, and the case narrowed to two principal issues. First was whether the government had done an adequate job assessing possible impacts of the exploratory drilling on endangered species. The agency persisted with the "paper transaction" argument. It said that leasing wouldn't jeopardize any threatened or endangered species, but confessed that it had insufficient information to know what exploration or extraction might do. It conceded that exploration would cause roads to be built through four of the five best grizzly bear valleys. It acknowledged that it knew little of how the exploration activities might affect eagles and falcons. The second major issue

was whether the Forest Service must list "not leasing" as one of the options it would consider in the course of analyzing the environmental impacts.

Judge Hatfield came down squarely on the side of the plaintiffs. He set aside the leases and ordered the government to issue no further leases until it complied with the federal laws in question. He wrote,

> The Deep Creek Area . . . of the Lewis and Clark National Forest is a rugged, remote and scenically varied terrain. . . . A dramatic series of deep escarpments and parallel valleys separates the Rocky Mountains from the northern high plains. . . . The geology of the area offers spectacular scenery. . . .

He didn't mention oil and gas until the ninth paragraph.

The government, egged on by Mountain States Legal Foundation, which had joined the case on behalf of several industrial interests, appealed the case. The Court of Appeals sided with Judge Hatfield, Volker, and the Bob Marshall Alliance.

These courtroom defeats did little to discourage the Forest Service, however. In 1981 it had announced that it was giving Getty Oil permission to build a road into the Little Granite Creek watershed of the Bridger-Teton National Forest, an area the Forest Service itself had recommended for wilderness designation. (Another name for the area is particularly fetching: Gros Ventre, or fat belly, for some presumably corpulent Indians that once frequented the area.) In this case, the Forest Service did prepare an environmental impact statement, but it had a subtle deficiency that Karin Sheldon was able to exploit for the benefit of keeping the place wild.

Getty Oil had held these leases for nearly a decade, the

Granite Creek and the Gros Ventre Mountains, Bridger-Teton National Forest, Wyoming.

Bear grass below the Chinese Wall, Bob Marshall Wilderness, Montana.

length of time such leases are supposed to run. When Getty asked permission to suspend its lease—to stop the clock before the lease expired—the Interior Department agreed, but included a requirement that future drilling in Little Granite Creek could be approved only if it would not have unacceptable impacts on the wilderness qualities of the area. Getty did not object to this provision, which authorized the Secretary of the Interior to deny the company's drilling permit applications. The Bureau of Land Management, however, forgot that the provision had been included and granted the company a drilling permit without even considering the alternative of saying no. Sheldon appealed the leasing decision to the Interior Department's Board of Land Appeals.

On July 20 the Board dismissed the appeal. The environmentalists ran to the Wyoming federal courthouse, where they were assigned to Judge Brimmer. It was something of a donnybrook. Counsel for the Jackson Hole Alliance was Jerry Spence, the kind of person newspapers tend to call "flamboyant." Spence had recently persuaded a jury to assess the nuclear-fuels manufacturing company Kerr-McGee some $10 million on behalf of the estate of Karen Silkwood and had also had a big win on behalf of a former Miss Wyoming who was described against her will in *Penthouse.* Mr. Spence's sartorial style ran to Central American shirts open to the navel and large quantities of Navajo jewelry (though not in the courtroom). Spence declared that he had joined the case "to drive the snakes from the Garden of Eden."

Karin Sheldon was the Legal Defense Fund's woman on the scene, on behalf of the Sierra Club and The Wilderness Society. The government had its fleet of lawyers, of course, as did Getty Oil. Judge Brimmer tolerated considerable wrangling in the court, listened to a great deal of testimony, and then threw the case back to the Board of Land Appeals and told it to try again.

The Board did so, canceling the drilling permit and telling the Bureau of Land Management to write a new environmental impact statement that would include "no drilling" as one of the possibilities. At this point Getty sued, and Sheldon and her colleagues intervened. This time their goal was to back up the government, whose dedication to defending victories like this one was certainly worth keeping an eye on in those days.

Being familiar with the dispute already, Judge Brimmer drew this case as well. The suit was technical, procedural, and intricate. It had little to do with mountains or streams or grizzly bears, and much to do with jurisdiction and authority. Getty argued that its leases were valid; the government had no right even to consider not letting it build a road and bore some holes. Karin Sheldon and her colleagues argued that a full investigation of the likely consequences of all feasible alternatives must include the alternative of leaving Little Granite Creek alone.

Judge Brimmer ruled in favor of the government and the conservationists. A telling blow had already been struck by Congress, which, while the case was being hashed out in Judge Brimmer's court, added Little Granite Creek to the existing Gros Ventre Wilderness. Congress acknowledged the case during debate over the bill and did not tell the judge how to rule, but public sentiment seemed clearly on the side of wilderness.

Palisades had been decided by the Court of Appeals for the District of Columbia Circuit in September of 1983. Judge Brimmer's opinion came out in the summer of 1985, and the Deep Creek decision appeared in May 1986. By all rights, these cases should have put the "paper transaction" argument to rest. Nonetheless, Deep Creek and Little Granite Creek found themselves the subjects of further appeals.

The appellate courts—the Ninth Circuit for Deep Creek, since it is in Montana, the Tenth for Little Granite, which is in Wyoming—stood firm. In both cases they agreed with the environmentalists that the government must insist on rigorous analysis of environmental impacts before it commits roadless areas to exploration for oil and gas.

The government decided not to appeal the Deep Creek decision. Not so the individual leaseholders in the Montana case and their stalwart counsel, the Mountain States Legal Foundation. They grimly asked the Supreme Court to review the case. The Supreme Court declined, and those wildlands remain, at least for now, free of roads and oil and gas rigs.

They will never, of course, be permanently free of the threat of those kinds of incursions until Congress is persuaded to set them aside as wilderness. When the price of petroleum begins once again to climb, as it surely will, the pressure to poke holes in wildlands will climb as well.

As this is written, the procedural fight is shifting, from specific oil and gas leases to long-range management plans for the national forests. These plans—a different one for each forest—will determine how much timber is cut, where oil and gas exploration will be permitted, how streams and fisheries will be protected, what indignities the grizzly will be expected to endure, and so on. And perhaps it's appropriate that oil and gas leasing be considered in the same context as logging of virgin forests. Both resources are limited and running out fast. Both industries that depend on those resources will soon have to adjust to a future that does not include so many gasoline-powered automobiles, so many houses and newspapers made from ancient timber. The fight now is over how we will preserve and protect the last remnants of those once-vast resources. Many long struggles lie ahead.

On the other side of the ledger, appreciation and recreational use of wilderness are growing at least as fast as demand for petroleum and timber. Pressure will mount on Congress to preserve these irreplaceable areas forever. Until that happens, litigators will be there to hold the fort.

CHAPTER SEVEN

On the Eastern Front
A Lake, a Wetland, a Forest, and a Valley

High on a tributary of the Hudson River, at the eastern edge of New York's magnificent Adirondack State Park, lies a glacier-carved lake called George. Named for England's George III, it figured prominently in the Revolutionary War, lying just south of Fort Ticonderoga where Ethan Allen and the Green Mountain Boys surprised the British in 1775. The elongated lake—thirty-three miles north to south and from less than a mile to three miles in width—has been a popular resort with New Yorkers for many years, attracting a summer population of many thousands. Visitors, and the handful of year-round residents, swim, boat, and fish in the lake, and draw their drinking and washing water from it.

It was no wonder, then, that the Adirondack Council, a citizen watchdog group, was concerned to learn in 1986 that the Lake George Park Commission—the state agency that manages the lake—had requested permission to dump a considerable amount of herbicide into the lake. The reason for the request was a small infestation of an exotic weed called European watermilfoil or spiked milfoil, which, in shallow lakes in warmer regions, has crowded out other plants and become a general nuisance. Milfoil was unknown in Lake George up to that time, and the Park Commission and the Lake George Association, a consortium of local property owners, wanted to eradicate the pesky weed immediately.

East shore of Lake George, Adirondack Park and Preserve, New York.

Fall color and birch trunks, Adirondack Park and Preserve.

Lake George and the Perils of Aquatic-Weed Control

Whether the milfoil was a recent arrival to Lake George or was simply being noticed for the first time was a matter of some dispute. Some said that since milfoil had been seen in nearby lakes since early in the century, it was unlikely that Lake George had been spared its presence until the 1980s. And since the extent of the milfoil infestation was so small—five or six acres of lake bottom out of a total of 28,000—it was far too early to call this a runaway blight demanding total warfare.

The proponents of herbicides argued that there was no evidence that the milfoil had arrived a minute before 1985. In that case, going from zero to six acres in two years was rapid growth indeed, and drastic measures were in order.

There are more ways than you'd think to tackle an infestation of aquatic weeds. One can drain the lake if it's a reservoir and parch the weeds to death. One can pull out the invaders by hand. Some success has been achieved by using an exotic fish called the grass carp, which has a voracious appetite but only slight ability to reproduce in cool water. Machines exist to shear weeds from lake bottoms. Dye can be put into lakes to blot out sunlight the plants need to grow. Likewise, mats can be fitted over beds of weeds to block sunshine. Finally, there's the chemical solution: dump strong poison on the plants and kill them that way.

Each of these various strategies has its pluses and minuses, depending on location, climate, and how much money there is to spend. The mechanical removal methods are by and large the most benign, but they're costly and must be repeated frequently. The light-blotting techniques are also without very serious side effects but are expensive as well. The carp are intriguing, but introducing exotic predators is always a risky business: they may eat things they're not supposed to eat. The herbicide solution is a very popular one because it works reasonably well and it's cheap.

The trouble is that the herbicides don't just kill the target weeds and then vanish. They can kill beneficial plants and other organisms as well. Then they drift away in ever more diluted form. In theory, they get so diluted as to pose no hazard to people who swim in or drink from the water. But, as with so many other chemical matters in the latter part of the twentieth century, we're beginning to understand that effects may be far more subtle, far harder to detect and predict, than we'd ever before have dreamed.

In any event, when the Adirondack Council learned of the Lake George Park Commission's request to douse several spots in Lake George with the herbicide Sonar, they went looking for a lawyer and found Howard Fox in the Legal Defense Fund's Washington, D.C., office. Fox is a native of the District who went to law school at New York University in Manhat-

Plants growing in frost-rived rock, the Tongue Range and the Narrows of Lake George, Adirondack Park and Preserve.

Lake George from Rogers Rock, Adirondack Park and Preserve.

tan. Following law school, he had presented himself at the Legal Defense Fund's door and worked as a volunteer until he was put on the payroll and eventually made a staff lawyer.

Before the commission could commence its plan to dump more than 6,000 pounds of Sonar across a little more than 100 acres of Lake George's bottom, it needed permission from the New York State Department of Environmental Conservation. A public hearing was scheduled, then postponed by the administrative law judge, Robert S. Drew. During the postponement period a conflict developed concerning the scope of issues to be considered at the hearing. The herbicide proponents argued that the hearing should be limited to whether the weed was really milfoil or something else, whether the agency planned to apply the chemical according to the manufacturer's suggestions, whether mats would be superior to the chemical, and whether the Sonar would unduly harm a native lake plant called *Nitella*. Nothing else.

Fox suggested that the scope of the agency's inquiry be broadened to include an investigation of whether the milfoil really posed such a threat that speedy action was warranted, whether there could be adverse effects on human health even if the herbicide were used as its manufacturer directed, whether there mightn't be other and preferable control techniques, and what effects on other organisms within the lake could be anticipated. The judge accepted Fox's suggestions.

With one thing and another, the hearing was pushed back until March 1987. One of the witnesses for the herbicide proponents was a man named Wilbur Dow, not of the chemical Dows, so far as is known, except by apparent inclination. This Dow owned a small fleet of imitation steamships that ply the waters of Lake George, and he didn't fancy seeing his paddlewheelers getting mired down in milfoil some years down the road. He regaled the courtroom with horrifying tales of how milfoil had clogged lakes from Florida to British Columbia, saying at one point that property owners at a certain lake in Canada were asking that their taxes be reassessed on a basis other than lake-front rates since the lake was gone, choked out by milfoil.

Dow was challenged repeatedly by Fox and by a lawyer for the state named Telisport Putsavage, known for obvious reasons as just plain Tel. He and Fox regularly caught Mr. Dow in his most flagrant exaggerations. At one point, Dow told the judge that he put Sonar in his coffee every morning, which evoked a warning from Putsavage that if that were true he could go to jail since Sonar was not licensed for use in New York State.

The star witness for the council was Dr. Ellen Silbergeld, a toxicologist with the Environmental Defense Fund. How her testimony came about is an interesting commentary on our complicated chemical world. Originally the terms of the hearing did not include any investigation of health effects of Sonar, since it had been registered for use in drinking-water reservoirs the previous year by the Environmental Protection Agency. A normal reaction to this situation is to presume that the agency had satisfied itself that the chemical itself was safe and that any breakdown products of it were safe as well.

Fox was not prepared to make that presumption. He acquired a list of the known breakdown products of Sonar, a few unpronounceable chemicals. Then he went looking for Ellen Silbergeld, who had provided toxicological assistance to the Legal Defense Fund on a previous lawsuit. Fox steamed into her office and asked if she could spot any problems on the list of Sonar's chemical progeny or, for that matter, with the way the manufacturer of Sonar had conducted its research.

Silbergeld scanned the documents Fox had brought and opined that the company seemed to have done an uncommonly thorough job of studying the direct health effects of Sonar. None of the breakdown products sounded ominous. "Are you sure?" Fox asked, determined not to let a possible catastrophic shred slip by unnoticed. He pushed gently: "Aren't any of the breakdown products dangerous?" Silbergeld scanned the list again. "Wait a minute," she said. "This MMF—monomethyl formamide—rings a faint bell." She turned to her computer and logged onto a service with a name like Toxline Database. She punched in MMF and hit pay dirt. Monomethyl formamide, said the computer, is highly teratogenic. In other words, it can cause severe malformations in fetuses. It is also persistent in water. It had been tested briefly as a treatment for liver cancer patients and had caused vomiting and a few deaths.

Jackpot. Fox quickly got on the phone with the head of the Bureau of Pesticide Management at the New York Department of Environmental Conservation to relay the news. She agreed to review carefully the material Fox would send. He then called the Environmental Protection Agency in Washington to investigate further. He wondered why the agency had not discovered this alarming fact during its registration review of Sonar. An official patiently explained that the agency simply doesn't have the time or resources to chase down every breakdown product of all the chemicals it must review. The chance of the agency's having come upon the troublesome MMF was "slim to none." As a general commentary on how the Environmental Protection Agency executes its responsibility, this admission has concerned some observers, but that's another story.

In any event, when the hearings finally commenced, on March 10, 1987, Fox and Silbergeld were armed with extensive documentation of the chemical problems associated with using Sonar in a drinking-water reservoir. After twenty-plus days of testimony and cross examination spreading across ten weeks, the park commission asked Judge Drew to put the matter on hold. Rather than submit briefs with final arguments, both on the facts and the law, they asked to take a break. The commission arranged for further studies, in cooperation with the state, of the speed with which the milfoil is spreading, if it's spreading at all. In late 1988 the commission tried to persuade Judge Drew to reopen the hearings, but the request was denied.

Meanwhile, an article in the British medical journal *The Lancet* had reported that DMF—a chemical cousin to MMF—

appeared to have caused testicular cancer in workers in a leather tannery in Gloversville, New York. Fox immediately asked the Environmental Protection Agency to order Sonar off the market, but the agency refused.

As Fox explained, "EPA's attitude is that herbicides are supposed to be poisons. They're meant to kill living things. It's extremely difficult in that situation to prove that something's so dangerous that it ought to be yanked off the market immediately." If further studies indicate that MMF or DMF derived from Sonar is a problem in drinking water, renewed attempts will surely be made to suspend the use of Sonar in reservoirs.

In early autumn 1989 the Lake George case was still hanging fire. The manufacturer of Sonar, chastened by the adverse publicity it received during the 1987 hearings, determined to conduct further studies on the health impacts of the herbicide. Having completed these studies, the company claimed that they showed a lack of identifiable health risks.

In the meantime, the final report of the milfoil survey emerged, and it contained new ammunition for Fox's efforts to protect the lake from Sonar. The report concluded that the area of dense milfoil beds in Lake George had increased from 1.39 acres in 1987 to 1.53 acres in 1988—an increase of only .14 acres out of a total lake surface area of 28,000 acres. As Fox observed, "In 1986 the pro-chemical forces were loudly proclaiming that a failure to treat Lake George with Sonar would, within three years, 'destroy the lake as we know it.' Well, to paraphrase Mark Twain's celebrated reaction upon reading his premature obituary, reports of the lake's death have been greatly exaggerated."

Indeed, Fox emphasized that the true threat to the lake's health comes from those who would use a blunderbuss approach to aquatic management, applying a chemical that would wind up killing not just the few scattered areas of milfoil, but also the adjoining stands of valuable native plants needed by the lake's ecosystem, including its abundant fish. "Our participation has already helped spur the use of two different non-chemical control methods in the lake. In 1986 a portion of the milfoil was covered with light-blocking mats that killed the plants underneath, and just recently a permit was granted for hand-pulling a significant portion of the remaining milfoil beds. It is our firm belief that these imaginative approaches offer the most promise for long-term intelligent management of milfoil in the lake."

Lake George is beset by other problems than the dubious profusion of an exotic aquatic weed. It shares the pressures that face all but the most remote venues around the world: too many people, too much waste, too much development, inclement atmospheric conditions. (Acid rain may well play a role in the success or failure of alien invaders like milfoil.) Yet if Lake George is to survive—both as a place for people to live and visit, and as an ecological unit—it must be proved that the introduction of a powerful synthetic poison will not do more harm than good. To that end, Howard Fox, the Adirondack Council, and the Sierra Club Legal Defense Fund have dedicated their efforts.

Baton rouge lichen on cypress trunks, Loxahatchee National Wildlife Refuge, Florida.

Big Cypress, the Everglades, and the Preservation of South Florida

The Everglades—Florida's famed "river of grass" wherein dwell alligators, panthers, Seminole Indians, and occasional fugitives from the law—became a national park in 1934. The Big Cypress swamp, a part of the Everglades ecosystem that might have been included in the park but wasn't, became a national preserve in 1973, both for its own sake and to protect the 'glades from environmental damage on its borders. Both have faced threats of one sort and another over the years, from poaching to desiccation caused by the diversion of water and disruption of the natural water cycle for agriculture and cities.

In the latter part of the 1980s Big Cypress had to cope with a situation that regrettably affects many units of the national park system and even more of the nation's wildlife refuges. Many parks and refuges have been acquired from private owners rather than carved out from lands already owned by the federal government. Often in such cases, the government will purchase the surface but leave in private hands the rights to any minerals that may exist underground. The practice has led to many conflicts, as one might expect, since the subsurface owner has the right to develop his underground holdings provided he doesn't cause too much disturbance to the surface. What constitutes "too much" disturbance has been a fertile field for litigation.

The problem arises as a result of the federal government's not having enough money to buy out mineral rights, and it winds up being a kind of Catch-22. If the minerals are thought to be meager or nonexistent, then the government can afford to buy them. But in that case, the threat of damage from a mineral developer is approximately nil. On the other hand, when serious damage is likely because minerals are thought to be abundant, the asking price is generally beyond the government's means. Thus the specter looms of roads and drilling rigs in sensitive wildlife refuges and other sorts of reserves that really ought to be managed mainly for wild creatures.

At some places the result has been disastrous, particularly at the D'Arbonne National Wildlife Refuge in northern Louisiana. There a gas developer has sterilized patches of refuge lands with brine and drilling mud, to the detriment of many creatures, including the red-cockaded woodpecker. Litigation brought by the Legal Defense Fund resulted in some protection for the birds, but a scandalously bad deed accepted by the Corps of Engineers when it bought the surface of the refuge, and a decidedly unfriendly federal judge, left the place still much at the mercy of the drillers.

At Big Cypress, whose 570,000 acres account for nearly half of the split-estate lands managed by the National Park Service, mineral rights are held principally by heirs of a grand railroad fortune. The Big Cypress Preserve was created principally from lands the federal government bought in the 1970s.

Like the Everglades to the south, Big Cypress is a maze of swamps and pinelands, bayous and sawgrass. It is fairly dry in winter and extremely wet in summer, when heavy rains and runoff from the north inundate all but the highest hardwood hammocks. It is, in a word, flat. The Big Cypress teems with fish and birds, and is the last refuge of the desperately endangered Florida panther, an original entry on the endangered species list. Once common from Texas to Tennessee to Florida, as few as thirty may now exist. They were driven to this perilous state by hunters for allegedly killing livestock.

Red-cockaded woodpeckers and endangered Cape Sable sparrows also inhabit the Big Cypress, along with a wide variety of plants and aquatic creatures in short supply elsewhere. Here, in the southwestern reaches of the Florida peninsula, is the last vestige of the Florida that existed for millennia prior to the arrival of Ponce de León in 1513, and the legions that followed him and tamed the landscape.

Over the years, man has inflicted exquisite misery on this land. Water diversion has led to terrible fires that have swept through the Big Cypress and the Everglades from time to time. Fire is a natural part of the life cycle in south Florida, but human meddling in the natural water cycle has contributed to fires more devastating than normal. Hunters have inflicted their own kind of harm on the inhabitants of the swamps as well. Off-road vehicles have left eroding ruts in the fragile marshes and uplands. Recently oil and gas exploration and development have added to the pressure on the preserve's resources.

The first deep exploratory well was sunk in south Florida in 1939. The first producing well went into service in 1943. At present there are two producing fields in the preserve, one in the far northwest corner and one on the northeastern edge. The southern half of the reserve, particularly a nearly pristine area known as "the loop," is about as wild a place as can be found in those parts, and is rapidly returning to pre-Colonial wilderness. Conservationists were therefore alarmed when an outfit called Shell Western Energy and Petroleum applied for permission to conduct extensive seismic surveys for petroleum in the refuge.

Shell asked permission from the Park Service to conduct seismic tests for oil and gas along eighty-five miles of line crisscrossing the preserve and running straight through the heart of the loop. Shell's plan was to detonate approximately 10,000 charges of dynamite at varying depths in holes drilled in the ground and then measure the resulting shock waves, a standard method of gauging potential petroleum deposits. The drilling and later detonation of explosive charges would require a good deal of floundering about in off-road vehicles, with attendant noise and commotion and destruction of plants and soil. There were worries about water pollution and interference with endangered species, which already face more adversity than they can cope with. At the very least, conservationists and the Park Service argued, a thorough and careful study of likely impacts of the exploration ought to be carried out prior to the activities.

Furthermore, they argued, Shell didn't have any business exploring for someone else's minerals in, or rather under, a federal preserve. Shell's agreement with the mineral owners did not oblige the company to reveal the results of its seismic testing.

Swamp lily and palms, Big Cypress National Preserve, Florida.

*The highly endangered Florida panther (*Felis concolor subspecies*). By Ted Schiffman/Peter Arnold, Inc.*

Shell would blast, measure, calculate, and then offer the owners a deal. It was likely that the owners would then take that offer to one of Shell's competitors and see if they could get a better deal. The second petroleum company would want to do its own testing, of course, so the reserve would have to suffer another 10,000 dynamite blasts.

These objections were communicated to and endorsed by William Penn Mott, the Director of the National Park Service, who had worked with Governor Ronald Reagan in California and came from the far more moderate wing of the Republican party. Mott's immediate boss, however, was Assistant Interior Secretary William Horn, who leaned more in the development direction. Horn directed the superintendent of Big Cypress to rush out a seventeen-page environmental assessment declaring that Shell's exploration would have no significant effect on the environment of the preserve—what's called in the trade a "negative declaration" or, like the hero of a TV sitcom of recent memory, a FONSI, or Finding of No Significant Impact.

The Park Service issued the FONSI and the permit to Shell. Bob Dreher, a staff attorney in the Legal Defense Fund's Washington, D.C., office, immediately filed suit in federal district court on behalf of The Wilderness Society and others, demanding that a full-blown environmental impact statement be prepared and questioning the propriety of giving an exploration permit to a commercial enterprise with no rights to any minerals it might find. It was April 22, 1988.

Meanwhile, it turned out, the regional director of the Park Service for south Florida, one Robert Baker, had written an angry memo to his boss, Bill Mott. The memo, dated December 23, 1987, read as follows:

> I want you to know that [Big Cypress] Superintendent Fagergren and I appreciate your efforts to convince the Assistant Secretary that the National Park Service undertake an environmental impact statement (EIS), on Shell Oil Company's proposal for seismic exploration in the Big Cypress National Preserve.
>
> As we all agreed during our meeting on Thursday, December 3, it was the prudent professional judgment to undertake the EIS, to explore all implications of the 85 miles of seismic exploration. It is unfortunate that the Assistant Secretary's office did not concur with our position and instructed us to issue the Environmental Assessment.
>
> What is troublesome is not only that the Park Service did not have the opportunity to explore all alternatives, i.e., hand-held drilling, feasibility of wider spacing of the holes, etc., but that the decision to go with an environmental assessment, which was a political decision, appears to be the National Park Service's proposal. Certainly the

Strangler fig, Everglades National Park, Florida.

Roosting herons (Ardea herodias)*, Loxahatchee National Wildlife Refuge.*

political leadership has the right to override our professional judgments, but I believe there should be a clear record of that decision.

One doesn't often find bravery of this order among public servants. Baker could easily have lost his job for writing such a memo, which found its way into the hands of a disbelieving but grateful Bob Dreher. Dreher's case was already strong; with the Baker memo it was airtight. He attached the memo to the papers he filed with the court and sent a copy to Secretary Horn.

Judge James W. Kehoe called for a hearing on Monday, May 9. At 5:15 P.M. on Friday the sixth, just as he was leaving his office to travel to Miami, Dreher's phone rang. It was the government's lawyer with big news: the Interior Department had just that afternoon rescinded its approval of the project, withdrawn the environmental assessment, and ordered Shell to cease operations in the preserve immediately. Dreher went home to his wife and children to spend an unexpected free weekend. It was one of the shortest cases in the history of the Legal Defense Fund.

Oil and gas exploration is far from the only threat to Big Cypress, and Shell remains interested in what lies beneath the preserve. No permit will be granted, however, without extensive advance studies to determine whether the drilling and blast-ing and off-road travel will do the kind of damage the biologists fear it will. Any permit is likely to require an agreement that all information gleaned from the testing be shared with the subsurface owner so that the exercise needn't be repeated.

Coincidentally, it was courage on the part of another government servant that sparked Legal Defense Fund activity on behalf of the Everglades, just south of Big Cypress, and the Loxahatchie National Wildlife Refuge to the east. There the main problem is not oil and gas development; it is water laden with fertilizers and pesticides that runs off canefields and citrus orchards through the refuge and into the 'glades. The polluted water has already damaged the refuge's flora and threatens its fauna; if drastic steps aren't taken soon, the Everglades will be next.

It is the responsibility of the state of Florida to control this pollution, but agricultural interests are powerfully entrenched and unenthusiastic about environmental-improvement measures that might cost them money. The state let the problem slide. Accordingly, the United States Attorney for South Florida, Dexter Lehtinen, filed suit against the state of Florida and its South Florida Water Management District in his capacity as defender of federal property—a national park and a national wildlife refuge. Florida growers and politicians were not pleased. The local water district retained high-priced Washington

*Sunset and palms, Big Cypress
National Preserve.*

Dry mud flat, a possible result of water diversion and desiccation, Everglades National Park.

counsel, and Dreher's clients feared that Lehtinen would be forced to drop the case. By the time Dreher heard what was going on, the heat on Lehtinen was getting near blister level. Dreher — on behalf of the Florida Audubon Society and several other conservation organizations — intervened in the suit virtually overnight, joining attorneys from the Environmental Defense Fund and other organizations. They made it clear they were prepared to take the case over should Lehtinen be forced to withdraw. Lehtinen was grudgingly allowed to proceed.

As of mid-1989, the case was anything but settled and promised to stretch on for many months or even years. There's little dispute over the inevitability of damage to the Everglades from agricultural runoff unless serious measures are taken to curb agricultural pollution. Just what those measures ultimately will be, and when they will begin, is not yet known.

More Than Just Timber

When the Pilgrims arrived at Plymouth Rock, the forests in the eastern part of what is now the United States were so dense that a squirrel could travel from Maine to Missouri without ever having to touch ground. To accomplish the same feat today, he'd have to hop a plane.

So rapid and thorough was the deforestation of the East — by both logging and blight — that by the time the Forest Service was established early in this century there was little left in the East worthy of national forest status. The forests had been leveled with no attempt to replant. Land had been turned to pasture, to farm, or left derelict; the loggers had moved West.

A useful example of this sorry history is Indiana. Prior to settlement by whites, the state was blanketed with wonderfully diverse forests, mostly deciduous hardwoods with a few evergreens thrown in. Much of the land was homesteaded and cleared for agriculture, the rest for saw timber. And it was cleared fast; in 1899 Indiana produced more timber than any other state. By the first years of the twentieth century, Indiana's forests were mostly memories, replaced by farms, some prosperous — many not. The land had been well suited for growing trees; it was not always so good for raising crops.

In the late 1920s, the Great Depression drove many Hoosier farmers into bankruptcy and off their farms. The federal government wound up being owner of large stretches of south-central Indiana as the homesteads failed and title to the land reverted to the government. The feds drew a line around a large section of it and called it the Hoosier National Forest, hoping the original forest would regenerate itself. The boundary encompassed about three-quarters of a million acres, although when the forest was established in 1935 only about 125,000 acres were in federal ownership. The majority of the land was acquired later.

The Forest Service let nature restore its ravaged landscape. Fifty years later, a thriving forest had been reestablished and was a much-prized recreation spot for people from Bloomington and nearby cities and towns. So when the Forest Service figured it was about time to log again, the citizenry objected. They did not want to see their forest go through another assault like the one of a century before.

The National Forest Management Act established an elaborate process for planning future management of the forests. That process includes extensive consultation between government officials and the general public. It is intended to produce long-range management plans that will both protect forest resources and provide timber and pulp and jobs. Julie McDonald, a Legal Defense Fund staff attorney, spent the better part of two years helping to draft regulations to implement the act. If the regulations were followed to the letter, the process ought to produce fair and balanced plans.

The law directed the Forest Service to produce plans for each of its hundred-plus forests by 1986. Unfortunately, federal agencies, particularly the environmental ones, seem institutionally unable to meet such deadlines, and the Forest Service did not confound that generalization. Draft plans began trickling out in the late 1970s, but the Reagan administration stopped the process and made the Forest Service start again, with greater emphasis on accelerated logging. Plans began to appear again in a few years, and by the middle of the 1980s most forests had draft plans out and circulating for comment.

Some say the planning process is a sophisticated device for keeping environmentalists and their legal counsel swamped in paperwork. (The Legal Defense Fund has participated in administrative appeals of upward of fifty forest plans during the 1980s.) It is, however, the only game in town, a game that must be played if the national forests are to get even a semblance of a fair shake, since it's certain that the timber industry is prepared to participate in the planning process every step of the way.

The draft management plan for the Hoosier was not one of the Forest Service's better efforts. It subjected almost the entire forest to clearcutting on a rotating basis over 80 to 120 years, which would have changed the composition of the forest from the native oak-hickory mix to poplar and other colonizing species. The plan relied on heavy applications of herbicides both for silvicultural purposes and to maintain openings for wildlife. It suggested dropping an existing ban against off-road vehicles. It called for extensive oil and gas development in the forest. It gave paltry protection to wildlife and to streams, especially those that run only part of the year.

The plan was released, and local citizens duly made their comments. The Forest Service duly ignored them. Citizens appealed to the chief. At this point, Eric Jorgensen, a young associate from the Legal Defense Fund's Washington office, a graduate of Harvard and the University of Virginia Law School, joined the fray as lawyer for the conservationists, who included the Sassafras Audubon Society, Forestwatch, the Hoosier Environmental Council, and local chapters of the better known national organizations.

When the Legal Defense Fund entered the picture, the Forest Service suggested that negotiations might be fruitful. Some modest progress was made, but then the regional forester quit and his replacement suspended the negotiations. The process had established, however, that the Hoosier plan was

Fall-colored maples, Charles C. Deam Wilderness, Hoosier National Forest, Indiana.

Forest pattern, Hoosier National Forest.

so bad, and the opposition to it so determined, that it would never survive the appeal intact.

In June 1987 the regional forester asked the chief to return the plan to him for revisions and suggested that the appeal could therefore be suspended. The chief complied, but he added a twist that has tainted the forest-planning process across the country: a plan is withdrawn for revisions, but in the interim the forest is managed as if the plan had been approved as written. It is a difficult position for conservationists, because frequently the status quo is even worse than a bad plan, so there's nowhere to turn. Jorgensen and his clients refused to accept either the status quo or the offending plan, and demanded protection for the forest during the revision of the plan. The Forest Service consented.

By August 1987 the Forest Service had concluded that the plan must be drastically revised, and shortly thereafter the forest supervisor was retired. The attitude of his replacement, Francis Voytas, represented a virtual turnaround. Voytas had cordial meetings with conservationists. They exchanged pleasant, forthright letters. In December 1987 Voytas issued an interim management directive for the forest that included most of what the conservationists had asked for the previous summer. Eric Jorgensen wrote a letter in January 1988, outlining improvements his clients would propose for the

directive, and Voytas adopted them verbatim.

Finally, in the spring of 1989, the new supervisor issued an outline for a new draft plan, to replace the one that had been appealed, and the transformation was nearly complete. Under the new plan, many roadless areas would be protected from logging, and overall timber harvest would be reduced by fifty percent. Clearcutting would be avoided in most cases. Bans on off-road vehicles, and the use of herbicides—adopted during negotiations over the draft plan—would remain. Protection for streams and wildlife—particularly for species dependent on old growth—would be strong. In all, it has the potential to be a fair, balanced, environmentally sensible plan, a far cry from what had been proposed originally.

Much attention focused on the Hoosier because it was the first plan issued for an eastern forest, and the Forest Service considered it a model for the rest of the region. Had the original plan become the blueprint for the Hoosier, it would have been grim news for other eastern forests. But fortunately, the Hoosier plan is likely to be something conservationists will be proud of and will point to as evidence that something as cumbersome and time-consuming as this planning process can actually work. Not only in the abstract, as a model for other plans, but also as a tool to protect as special a place as the Hoosier National Forest.

Wildlife Versus Electricity in Canaan Valley

Canaan Valley, in the northeastern corner of West Virginia, is a broad, rolling depression high on the Appalachian Plateau. When the glaciers from the most recent ice age receded, they left behind a few islands in the Appalachian Mountains that more closely resemble ecosystems in Canada and New England, hundreds of miles to the north, than their immediate surroundings. Canaan Valley is one such place.

Canaan Valley contains the biggest wetland in West Virginia, the only state in the union with not a single national wildlife refuge within its borders. The valley encompasses 28,000 acres—fourteen miles long by four miles wide, give or take—and is "canoe-shaped," according to the newspaper writers of the day. It runs more or less north and south and is drained by several forks of the Blackwater River. The outflow from the valley runs through a gap in the surrounding mountains to the west. The gap is narrow; just the sort of place dam engineers adore.

Within the valley are sumptuous marshes and bogs, swamps, fens, and mires. They are home to beaver by the score, plus bear and deer and dozens of other creatures that feed on the cranberries and other delicacies our much-abused wetlands produce in profusion. At least 590 species of mainly boreal plants exist in the valley—that is to say, plants more commonly found in the northerly lands of Canada. More than 150 species of birds live there or visit during migration. Many people enjoy the valley as hunters, fishermen, hikers, and skiers. Others think its best use would be as a generator of electricity. The idea has been around a good long time. In the 1920s, power-company representatives began quietly buying land in the middle of the valley, much of it in the parts too wet and boggy to be of any use for farming or commercial development. They also acquired a plot on the top of Cabin Mountain, a long ridge that divides Canaan Valley from the Dolly Sods Wilderness immediately to the east. Fifty years later their plans would crystallize and become known. Those plans would spark one of the longer legal battles in the annals of environmental litigation; at the time the present account was written, there was no way to tell whether the fight was nearly finished, at its midpoint, or just beginning.

Electricity is a wonderful thing. Indeed, only two substantial drawbacks to electricity spring easily to mind. First, it must be generated, which has considerable cost no matter how it is done. Second, it cannot be stored in large quantities. Science has yet to find us a way to fill up a barrel with electricity to put in the attic against the next time the power fails. Not that science hasn't tried.

One rather clumsy attempt to outsmart this problem is called pump-storage. Two reservoirs are built, one above the other, with a pipe connecting the outflow of the upper reservoir to turbines at the intake of the lower one. When demand for power is high, water is released from above, rushes down through the powerplant, and generates power that hums through the wires to run air conditioners and all-electric kitchens. When demand drops, power from another plant—most likely burning coal or oil, even uranium—is used to pump the water back up through the pipe to the topside holding pond. It is ingenious, but scandalously inefficient. For every two kilowatts of power generated at the plant, three kilowatts must be used to pump the water back uphill. Still, the demand for power fluctuates so wildly that the gross waste of power can sometimes be justified. When it can, power developers begin looking around for likely sites. Often they provoke controversy, as at Canaan Valley.

In June 1970 a consortium of three nearby power companies called Allegheny Power System asked the Federal Power Commission for permission to build the Davis Power Project, a pump-storage power facility in Canaan Valley. It would consist of a 7,000-acre reservoir behind a dam at the valley's outlet, which would submerge 4,000 of the valley's 6,000 acres of wetlands. The storage tank would be a 500-acre reservoir right on top of Cabin Mountain, in a natural basin whose sides would be built up so that when need demanded, the surface of the upper reservoir would drop nearly sixty feet. The Davis Power Project would be capable of generating 1,000 megawatts.

As is usual in projects like this, the promoters dressed their proposal up with extra added attractions. The lower reservoir would be a great new recreational resource for Tucker County, they said. Now, reservoirs are always being touted as great for swimming and boating and the like, but they often have a problem with their shorelines. The fluctuating level of the lake surface tends to leave lifeless and unsightly mudflats and silt-banks where one might expect beaches or thriving marshes. The lower reservoir of the Davis project, whose surface would bounce up and down by four feet every time the switch was pulled, would seem certain to suffer this problem. But Allegheny was ready. In a brochure the company produced to win friends for its project, it made the following claim: "Because the fluctuations in the pool level are on a more or less regular basis, it is possible that an interesting new natural area may develop —a freshwater tidal zone." If only it were that easy.

The Fish and Wildlife Service, meanwhile, had another idea for Canaan Valley. It proposed acquiring all 28,000 acres of it for a national wildlife refuge. But before any steps could be taken toward that end, the power commission in 1974 held hearings on Allegheny's application, hearings that lasted ten weeks. Ron Wilson of the Legal Defense Fund represented a variety of conservation groups that opposed the project passionately. They testified and organized and cajoled and lobbied. They could not make much progress toward swaying public opinion in Tucker County, which felt it needed the jobs and money the Davis project would, in theory, bring in, but they mobilized conservationists nationally against the project and explained how Tucker County could improve its lot without ruining the valley.

They persuaded the staff of the FPC to oppose the project

Early snowfall in the northern Canaan Valley, West Virginia.

as well, including the agency's administrative law judge, who considered arguments on all sides of the proposition. In February 1975 the staff formally recommended that the commission reject the permit application.

Two years later, on April 21, 1977, the commission ignored its staff and, by a vote of two to one, approved Allegheny's permit application. The deciding vote was cast by a little-known commissioner by the name of James G. Watt.

Eight months later, after several requests for reconsideration were rejected by the commission, Ron Wilson filed suit in the Court of Appeals for the District of Columbia Circuit in an attempt to invalidate the permit. This was in January 1978. Petitioners in the case, in addition to local and national conservation groups, included the state of West Virginia and the federal Department of the Interior.

Another two months passed. The Fish and Wildlife Service issued a draft environmental impact statement describing its plan to buy out the power companies and create a wildlife refuge in the valley. And four months after that, the U.S. Army Corps of Engineers got into the act. The promoters of the Davis project had applied to the Corps for a permit, required by the Clean Water Act, to dredge and fill material within a navigable waterway: in this case to dam a river and destroy thousands of acres of wetlands.

In July 1978 the Corps denied the permit. The power companies filed their own suit, arguing that the Corps had no jurisdiction over the project anyway, since it had already been approved by the Federal Power Commission, by then rechristened the Federal Energy Regulatory Commission. Defenders of Canaan Valley, represented again by Ron Wilson and the Legal Defense Fund, intervened in the new lawsuit on the side of the Corps.

Canaan Valley was by this time attracting a considerable amount of attention. In February 1979, President Carter appointed a task force to try to find a way to avoid building the Davis project and still provide the power the various interests said they needed. Yet another round of hearings began, yet another set of chores for Wilson and his clients. The presidential task force report found that there were better ways to produce power than the Davis project, and recommended against it.

Around this time, the energy commission too seemed to have second thoughts. It asked the Court of Appeals to send the matter back to the agency for reconsideration. The court, for unexplained reasons, refused. It had put matters on hold pending the outcome of the suit against the Corps. In December 1980, the judge in the case involving the Corps of Engineers ruled that the Corps had no jurisdiction over the project, that

Wetlands, Canaan Valley.

the Federal Power Act preempted the Federal Water Pollution Control Act. It was a serious setback.

A month later, Ronald Reagan was sworn in as President, and James Watt, who had been instrumental in keeping the Canaan Valley power project alive when he served on the Federal Power Commission, took over as Secretary of the Interior. One of his first acts in office was to stop spending any money to acquire new land for national parks or wildlife refuges. So the Fish and Wildlife Service's plan to buy the valley for a refuge was dead.

In February 1981, Wilson and his colleagues appealed the judge's decision in the suit against the Corps. It was assigned to the same three judges who had heard arguments in the conservationists' suit against the Federal Power Commission two years earlier. At this point, for unknown reasons, the pace of events, already glacial, ground to a virtual halt. Arguments in the appeal were conducted in June 1982, and the long wait began. Finally, on January 13, 1987, the Court of Appeals released its opinion. That's four and a half years

after oral argument; the usual period is a few months.

The wait, however, was worth it. The conservationists won. The Corps did indeed have jurisdiction over the project, and the Corps had said no dam. The Supreme Court later that year declined to review the case. But still there was no tidy end of the story. The original suit against the Corps had made several other assertions that the court had not dealt with, so the case went back to the judge for further proceedings. The struggle could continue for years, since the power company has shown little interest in selling its holdings, even as the federal government once again begins spending a little money on land acquisition.

Power demand had leveled off as of this writing, though, and it was considered unlikely that the power companies would want to spend the large amount of money needed to build the project even if they could get permission. By mid-1989 Ron Wilson had spent the better part of fifteen years battling the Davis Power Project and was fully prepared to spend another fifteen, if that's what it would take.

Bird nests in trees, late autumn in Canaan Valley.

Hamilton Creek and Valhalla, Sequoia National Park, California.

Afterword

The Sierra Club Legal Defense Fund was conceived in the middle 1960s, incorporated in March 1970, and opened its doors for business in August 1971. It has, in the ensuing twenty years, become a major force in environmental affairs in the United States. It started with two attorneys in San Francisco. That office rapidly grew to three, then four, then five lawyers, taking on cases both nearby and at some distance. In 1972 an office was opened in Denver to take on more work in the Rockies and the Colorado Plateau.

Nineteen seventy-eight saw the opening of offices in Juneau and Washington, D.C. The Seattle office opened in 1987 and the Honolulu operation began in 1988. As the next decade begins, plans are being made to open offices in the Southeast and the Midwest in the near future. Thought is also being given to expanding to Canada, and Legal Defense Fund lawyers are beginning to take on cases that cross national frontiers.

H. Donald Harris, Jr., was the organization's first president, and served until late 1989, when he became treasurer. Harris and R. Fredric Fisher, the Legal Defense Fund's first vice president, served on the Sierra Club's volunteer Legal Committee in the 1960s. They had filed many lawsuits and administrative appeals on the club's behalf, on a wide variety of matters from timber sales to Grand Canyon dams. The two lawyers are given much of the credit for creating the organization and shepherding it through its first two decades.

James Moorman was the first executive director; he served in that capacity for three years, then became a staff lawyer to concentrate on litigation. John Hoffman, previously a staff lawyer, held the position of executive director from 1974 to 1977. Moorman left the Legal Defense Fund that year to join the Carter administration and Hoffman went into private practice in San Francisco. John Hoffman continues to serve on the organization's Board of Trustees.

The third, and still serving, chief executive is Fredric P. Sutherland, known to all as Rick. A lawyer himself, he was a cofounder of the Center for Law in the Public Interest in Los Angeles in 1971. He assumed leadership of the Sierra Club Legal Defense Fund in 1977. Sutherland has presided over the organization's years of dramatic growth. When he took over, there were two offices, five attorneys, and a budget of $451,000. At the beginning of 1990, there were six offices with two more expected imminently, twenty-five full-time lawyers and many others on retainer or working part time. Staff also included the executive director, coordinator attorney, clerks, paralegals, resource specialists, support staff, and a vigorous development department. The budget was nudging $7 million.

The Legal Defense Fund does not have members as such, but it does have approximately 120,000 individual supporters, making it one of the half-dozen largest citizen environmental organizations in the country.

As the Legal Defense Fund approaches its twentieth anniversary, it continues to expand to meet the needs of its clients. Although this involves change—more offices, more personnel, more modern technology—the mission remains the same: to provide the highest possible quality of legal advocacy to the conservation movement.   —T. T.

Water lilies, Loxahatchee National Wildlife Refuge, Florida.

Trustees of the Sierra Club Legal Defense Fund 1971–1989

Clients Represented by the Sierra Club Legal Defense Fund

Adirondack Council, New York

Alabama Coastal Alliance

Alabama Conservancy

American Federation of State, County, and
   Municipal Employees

American Fisheries Society

American Littoral Society

American Lung Association of Hawaii

American Rivers Conservation Council

American Wilderness Alliance

Ancient Forest Defense Fund, California

Animal Protection Institute of America

Arizona Wildlife

Arizonans for a Quality Environment

Atlantic Salmon Federation, Maine

Beaverhead Forest Concerned Citizens, Montana

Bighorn River Watershed Coalition, Montana

Boot 'n Blister Club, California

California Coalition for Alternatives to Pesticides

California Council for Survival Resources

California Native Plant Society

California Trout

California Wilderness Coalition

Cenaliulriit Coastal Management District, Alaska

Chemehuevi Tribe of Indians, Arizona

Citizens Against Refinery Effects, Virginia

Citizens Against Rocky Flats Contamination, Colorado

City of Angoon, Alaska

City of Aurora, Colorado

City of Colorado Springs, Colorado

Cochise Conservation Council, Arizona

Colorado Environmental Coalition

Colorado Mountain Club

Colorado Open Space Council

Columbia Gorge United, Oregon

Committee for Green Foothills, California

Confederation of Indian Nationalities of the
   Ecuadorian Amazon

Conservation Council for Hawaii

Conservation Foundation

Conservation Law Foundation of New England

Coral Reef Society

Council of the Southern Mountains

Defenders of Wildlife

Denali Citizens Council, Alaska

Desert Protective Council, California

Desert Survivors, California

Endangered Species Committee of California

Environmental Defense Fund

Environmental Policy Institute

Environmental Protection Information Center, California

Federation of Western Outdoor Clubs

Florida Audubon Society

Florida Defenders of the Environment

Florida Wildlife Society

Forest Watch, Indiana

Friends of Berner's Bay, Alaska

Friends of Santa Paula Creek, California

Friends of Sierra Valley, California

Friends of the Columbia River Gorge, Oregon

Friends of the Earth

Friends of the Everglades, Florida

Friends of the Horsepasture, North Carolina

Friends of the River Foundation, California

Friends of the Sea Otter, California

Frontera Audubon Society

Get Oil Out, California

Greenpeace International

Greenpeace USA

Griffin Bay Preservation Committee

Hawaii Audubon Society

Headwaters, Oregon

High Peaks Audubon Society, New York

Holy Cross Wilderness Defense Fund, Colorado

Hoosier Environmental Council, Indiana

Huachuaca Audubon Society, Arizona

Huaorani Indians, Ecuador

Humane Society of the United States

Idaho Conservation League

Idaho Sportsmen's Coalition

Indiana League of Women Voters

International Indian Treaty Council

Izaak Walton League of America

Jackson Hole Alliance, Wyoming

Jefferson Valley Sportsmen, Montana

Kentucky Conservation Committee

Kitsap Audubon Society, Washington

League for Coastal Protection

League to Save Lake Tahoe

Life of the Land, Hawaii

Los Angeles Audubon Society

Manor Area Neighbors Organization, Texas

Marianas Audubon Society, Guam

Maricopa Audubon Society, Arizona

Maryland Conservation Council

Mendocino Unified School District, California

Mobile Audubon Society, Alabama

Mono Lake Committee, California

Monroe County Humane Society, Indiana

Montana Wilderness Association

Mount Diablo Audubon Society, California

National Audubon Society

National Coalition Against the Misuse of Pesticides

National Outdoor Leadership School

National Parks and Conservation Association

Native Village of Minto, Alaska

Natural Resources Council of Maine

Natural Resources Defense Council

Nebraska Wildlife Federation

Nevada Outdoor Recreation Association

New York Zoological Society

North Cascades Conservation Council, Washington

North Gulf Oceanic Society, Alaska

Northcoast Environmental Center, California

Northern Alaska Environmental Center

Northern Plains Resources Council, Montana

Northwest Coalition for Alternatives to Pesticides, Oregon

Northwest Environmental Defense Center, Oregon

Northwest Rivers Alliance

Nunam Kitlutsisti, Alaska

Okanogan Wilderness League, Washington

Olijato Chapter of the Navajo Tribe, Arizona

Oregon Natural Resources Council

Oregon Nordic Club

Oregon Student Public Interest Research Group

Oregon Trout

Pacific Coast Federation of Fishermen's Associations

Park County Resource Council, Wyoming

People Against Chlordane

People for Open Space, California

Pilchick Audubon Society, Washington

Planning and Conservation League, California

Portland Audubon Society, Oregon

Prescott Audubon Society, Arizona

Preserve Area Ridgelands Committee, California

Project Jonah

Project Land Use, California

Protect Our Waters and Environmental Resources, Washington

Public Citizen Litigation Project, Washington, D.C.

Puget Sound Alliance, Washington

Rainforest Action Network

Red Mesa Chapter of the Navajo Tribe, Arizona

Resources Center, California

Sassafras Audubon, Indiana

Save Our Aquatic Resources and Environment, Florida

Save San Francisco Bay Association

Save the Dunes, Alabama

Scenic Shoreline Preservation Conference, California

Seattle Audubon Society, Washington

Service Employees International Union

Sierra Club

Sitka Conservation Society, Alaska

Siuslaw Task Force, Oregon

Society for Animal Protective Legislation

Sonomans for Gentle Growth, California

Southern California Alliance for Survival

Southern Utah Resource Council

Southern Utah Wilderness Alliance

Texas Committee on Natural Resources

The Wilderness Society

Tropical Audubon Society, Florida

Trout Unlimited

Trust for Public Land

Tucson Audubon Society, Arizona

Utah Wilderness Association

Village of Birch Creek, Alaska

Virgin Islands Conservation Society

Washington Environmental Council

Washington Native Plant Society

We Care Austin, Texas

West Virginia Highlands Conservancy

Western Nebraska Resources Council

Western River Guides Association

Western Sanders County Involved Citizens, Montana

Whale Center, California

Wyoming Outdoor Coordinating Council

Fall-colored geranium leaves and aspen trunk, The Palisades, Targhee National Forest, Idaho.

Sierra Club Legal Defense Fund Offices

San Francisco Office
2044 Fillmore Street
San Francisco, California 94115
415-567-6100

Washington, D.C. Office
1531 P Street N.W., Suite 200
Washington, D.C. 20005
202-667-4500

Alaska Office
325 Fourth Street
Juneau, Alaska 99801
907-586-2751

Rocky Mountain Office
1631 Glenarm Place, Suite 300
Denver, Colorado 80202
303-6233-9466

Pacific Northwest Office
216 First Avenue South, Suite 330
Seattle, Washington 98104
206-343-7340

Mid-Pacific Office
212 Merchant Street, Suite 202
Honolulu, Hawaii 96813
808-599-2436

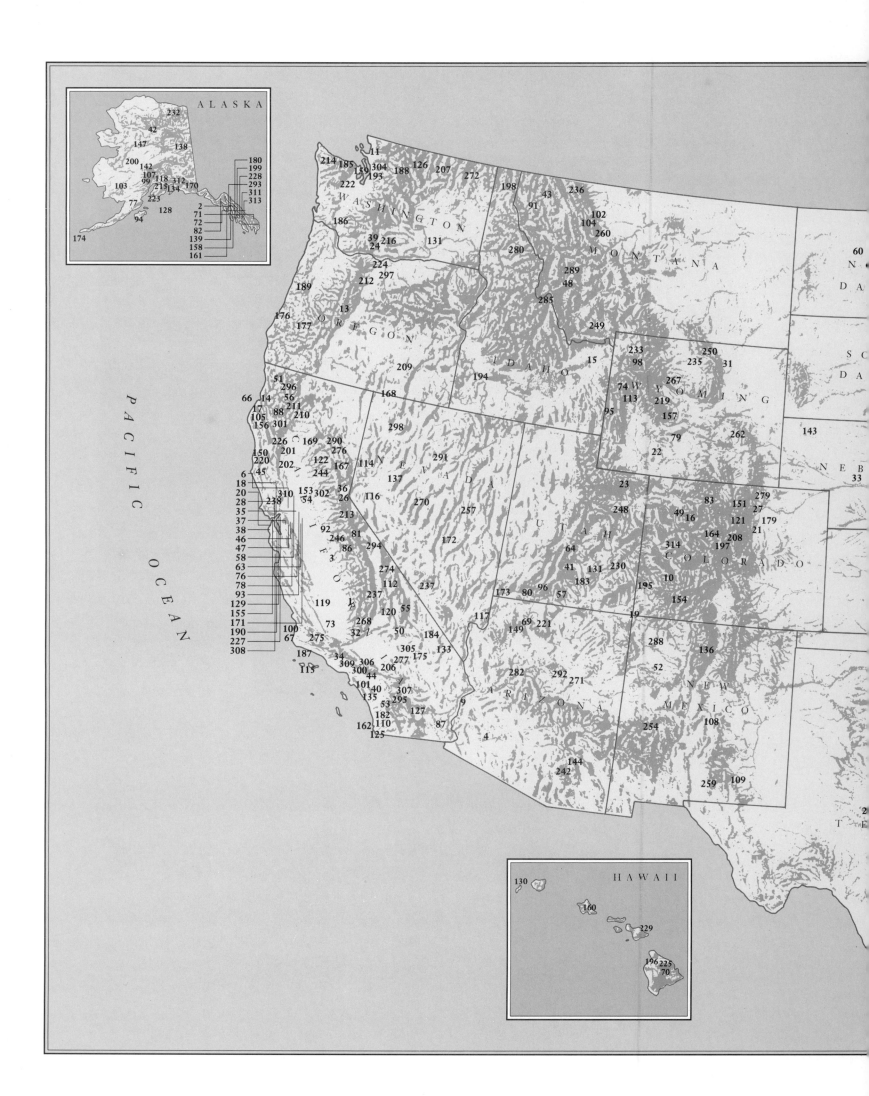

ALASKA

232
42
147
138
200 142
107 118 312 180
99 228 170 199
103 223 134 228
77 312 293
128 311
94 2 313
174 71
72
82
139
158
161

PACIFIC OCEAN

214 185 11
222 159 304 188 126 207 272
193
186
39 216 131
24
224
212 297
189
176 13
177 OREGON
51 209
296 168
66 14 56
17 88 211
105 210
156 301 298
226 169 290
150 201 276
220 202 122 167 114 NEVADA
6 244 291
18 36 137
20 310 302 116
28 153 26
35 238 54 270
37 213 257
38
46 92 172
47 246 81
58 86 294
63 274
76 237
78 112
93 237 55
129 119 120
155 73 50
171 32 305 184
190 100 275 277 175 133
227 67 34 306 206
308 187 309 300 44
115 101 40 307
135 53 295
182 127 9
110 87
162
125 4

WASHINGTON
304
198 236
43
91
280 289
48
285
249
15
233 250
98 235 31
74 267
113 219
95 157
79 262
22
23
248 83 151 279
49 16 121 27 179
314 164 208 21
41 131 230 197
64 183
173 80 96 10
57 195 154
19
117
149 69 221
288 136
282 52
292 271
254 108
MONTANA

N.
DA

S.
DA

143

NEB
33

60

UTAH
COLORADO

ARIZONA NEW MEXICO
144 259 109
242

HAWAII
130
160
229
196 225
70

150

Cases Brought by the Sierra Club Legal Defense Fund

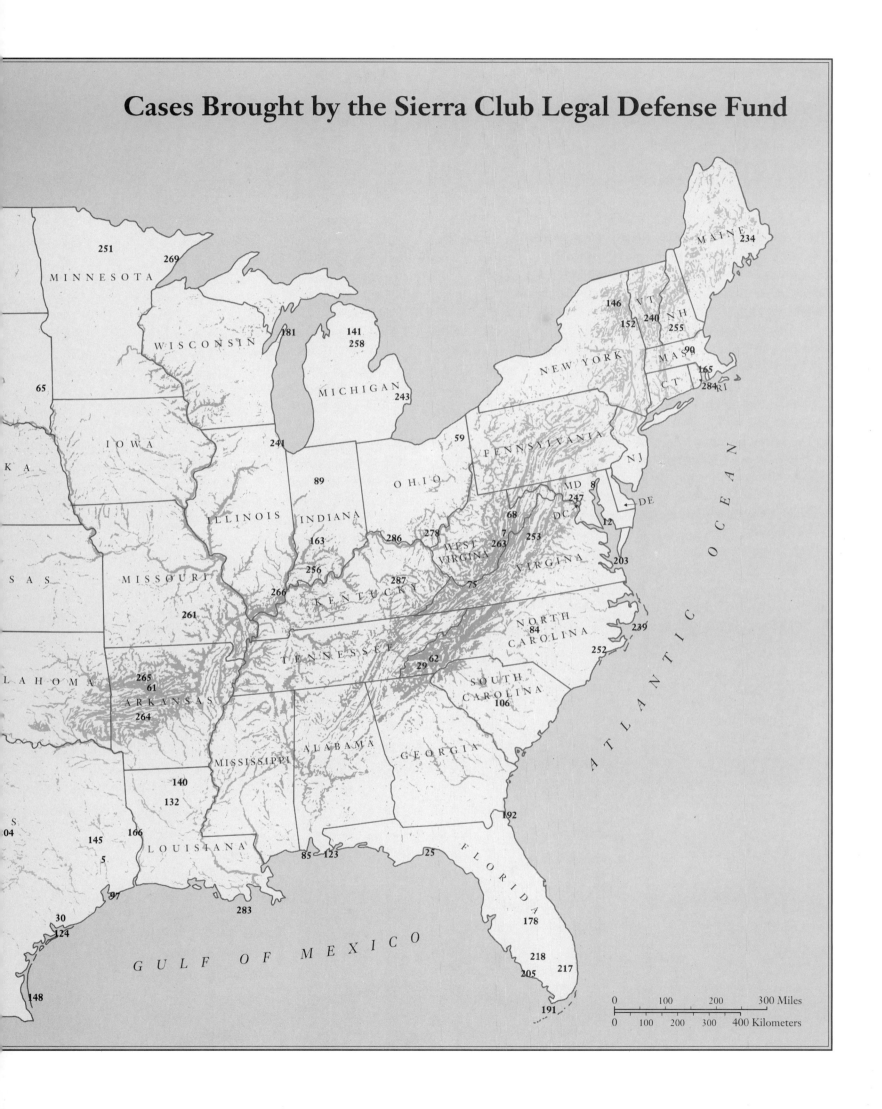

MINNESOTA 251 269

WISCONSIN 181

MICHIGAN 141 258 243

MAINE 234

146 VT 240 NH 255

152

NEW YORK

MASS 90

165

CT 284 RI

65

IOWA 241

ILLINOIS 89

INDIANA 163

256

PENNSYLVANIA

59

OHIO

NJ

MD 8

247

DC

12

68

7 253

WEST 263

VIRGINIA

DE

203

VIRGINIA

KA

SAS

MISSOURI

261

286 278

266 287 75

KENTUCKY

NORTH 84

CAROLINA 239

LAHOMA

265

61

ARKANSAS

264

TENNESSEE

29 62

252

SOUTH

CAROLINA

106

S

04

145 166

5

140

132

MISSISSIPPI ALABAMA

GEORGIA

192

LOUISIANA

85 123

25

FLORIDA

97

283

178

30

124

218

205 217

GULF OF MEXICO

148

191

ATLANTIC OCEAN

0   100   200   300 Miles

0 100 200 300 400 Kilometers

Map Legend

We present this map to give an overall impression of the geographic diversity of the cases the Legal Defense Fund has carried during its first twenty years. The impression is accurate, but it requires some words of explanation.

It is not complete. It leaves out several dozen national cases—cases involving acid rain, dust, and other air pollutants; cases involving specific herbicides and other water pollutants; cases concerning the transfer of management jurisdiction from one agency to another; cases brought to establish water rights for wilderness and wildlife; cases filed to prevent deterioration of air quality; a case to stop the elimination of several hundred roadless areas from wilderness consideration; and others.

It is incomplete in another respect as well. Some of the entries represent multiple cases. At Admiralty Island in Alaska, for example, the Legal Defense Fund brought more than two dozen lawsuits and administrative appeals. At Lake Tahoe, a

half-dozen. And some cases don't appear on the map because they lie outside the range of the map itself, cases involving Guam, Puerto Rico, the Virgin Islands, and Ecuador.

The concentration of cases in the West is a product of the fact that the first two offices of the organization were situated in that region, in San Francisco and Denver. This in turn is because the bulk of the public lands, lands managed by the National Park Service, Forest Service, Bureau of Land Management, and Fish and Wildlife Service are located in the West. It is these lands that the Legal Defense Fund has spent much of its effort defending.

The gaps on the map exist in part because there are vigorous, committed, successful private attorneys or nonprofit organizations in those areas that have represented conservation interests well. Particularly noteworthy are the Conservation Law Foundation of New England and the Southern Environmental Law Center in Virginia and North Carolina.

Key to Map of Cases

1. Mineral King, California. *Ski resort in wilderness.*

2. Admiralty Island, Alaska. *Clearcutting in wilderness.*

3. Central Valley, California. *Federal irrigation policy.*

4. Gila River, Arizona. *Brush clearing, wildlife habitat.*

5. Wallisville Dam, Texas. *Dam and canal project.*

6. California Water Project. *Peripheral canal, Tracy pumping plant.*

7. Otter Creek, West Virginia. *Wilderness threatened.*

8. Baltimore, Maryland. *Expressway planned through city park.*

9. Chemehuevi Indian Reservation, Arizona. *Suit to protect water quality.*

10. Uncompahgre Primitive Area, Colorado. *Forest Service forced to consider wilderness designation.*

11. Cherry Point, Washington. *Oil transfer facility.*

12. Chesapeake Bay, Maryland. *Park established as mitigation for liquid natural gas facility.*

13. Red Creek, Oregon. *Appeal of timber sale in roadless area.*

14. Redwood National Park, California. *Forced expansion of park.*

15. Teton Dam, Idaho. Dam.

16. East Meadow Creek, Colorado—*landmark case requires Forest Service to consider wilderness before logging.*

17. Cape Mendocino, California. *Beach access for public.*

18. San Francisco Bay, California. *Public access, wetlands protection.*

19. Four Corners, New Mexico. *Tall stacks.*

20. Highway 1, California. *Expansion of scenic highway.*

21. Arapaho National Forest, Colorado. *Access to mining claim.*

22. Rock Springs, Wyoming. *Jim Bridger Power Plant.*

23. Uinta Mountains, Utah. *Current Creek dam.*

24. Mount Adams Wilderness, Washington. *Timber sale in proposed wilderness.*

25. Wetlands, Florida and Louisiana. *Offshore oil drilling.*

26. Kirkwood Meadows, California. *Private ski development on public land.*

27. Boulder, Colorado. *New highway through town.*

28. San Francisco Bay, California. *Leslie Salt ponds.*

29. Joyce Kilmer Wilderness, North Carolina. *Highway through wilderness.*

30. Matagorda Bay, Texas. *Two dams.*

31. Douglas to Gilette, Wyoming. *Rail line for coal.*

32. Tejon Ranch, California. *Development in condor habitat.*

33. Sutherland, Nebraska. *Coal-fired powerplant.*

34. Santa Paula Creek, California. *Stream channelization.*

35. Mount Diablo, California. *Sand-silica mining.*

36. Lake Tahoe, California. *Planning and growth.*

37. Hayward, California. *Freeway expansion.*

38. Half Moon Bay, California. *Country club development*

39. Cold Springs, Washington. *Timber sale, road construction.*

40. Long Valley, California. *Herbicides for brush clearing.*

41. Circle Cliffs, Utah. *Road through national park.*

42. Arctic National Wildlife Refuge, Alaska. *Natural gas pipeline.*

43. Mt. Henry, Montana. *Clearcutting.*

44. North Legg Lake, California. *Wildlife habitat destruction.*

45. Sea Ranch, California. *Construction on coast.*

46. Blackhawk Ranch, California. *Second-home development.*

47. Apperson Ridge, California. *Guest ranch.*

48. Moose Creek, Montana. *Clearcutting and road construction.*

49. Beaver Creek, Colorado. *Ski development.*

50. California desert. *Off-road motorcycle racing.*

51. Blue Creek, California. *Gasquet-Orleans road.*

52. Mount Taylor, New Mexico. *Mineral exploration road.*

53. San Marcos, California. *Annexation of wild land.*

54. Consumnes River, California. *Float trip as trespassing.*

55. Death Valley, California. *Strip mining in national monument.*

56. Six Rivers National Forest, California. *Timber Management Plan; geologic hazards.*

57. Kaiparowits Plateau, Utah. *Coal mine and powerplant.*

58. Solano County, California. *Air pollution & factories.*

59. Mahoning Valley, Ohio. *Steel industry water pollution.*

60. *Whooping crane critical habitat.*

61. Ozark-St. Francis National Forest. *Herbicides & type conversion.*

62. Standing Indian Mountain, North Carolina. *Road building and clearcutting.*

63. Sacramento River, California. *Dow Chemical plant.*

64. Castle Valley, Utah. *Intermountain Power Project.*

65. Eastern South Dakota. *Rural water hookups.*

66. Humboldt Bay, California. *Nuclear plant decommissioning.*

67. Point Conception, California. *Liquefied natural gas plant.*

68. Canaan Valley, West Virginia. *Davis Power Project.*

69. Grand Canyon, Arizona. *Pollution by river-runners.*

70. Mauna Kea, Hawaii. *The endangered palila.*

71. Misty Fjords, Alaska. *Molybdenum mine.*

72. Tongass National Forest, Alaska. *Alaska Lumber and Pulp.*

73. Kern County, California. *County general plan.*

74. Jackson, Wyoming. *Airport expansion in national park.*

75. Brumley Gap, Virginia. *Pump-storage project in wetland.*

76. Coyote Creek, California. *Highway.*

77. National monuments, Alaska. *State challenge to Carter Antiquities Act withdrawals.*

78. Hayward, California. *Agricultural land preservation.*

79. BLM lands, Wyoming. *RMOGA oil and gas leasing.*

80. Allen-Warner Valley, Utah. *Coal powerplants.*

81. Mono Lake, California. *Water rights, relicted lands.*

82. Chilkat River, Alaska. *Logging and bald eagles.*

83. Williams Fork, Colorado. *Water diversion.*

84. Wilderness, North Carolina. *Forest Service management.*

85. Dauphin Island, Alabama. *Barrier island preservation.*

86. San Joaquin River, California. *Hydro projects in wilderness.*

87. Imperial Dunes, California. *Offroad vehicles.*

88. Mendocino County, California. *Aerial herbicides.*

89. Indiana. *State Implementation plan and acid rain.*

90. Acton, Massachusetts. *Toxic contamination.*

91. Cabinet Mountains, Montana. *Grizzly bears.*

92. Stanislaus River, California. *Dam.*

93. Mt. Tamalpais, California. *TV transmission tower.*

94. Terror Lake, Alaska. *Dam.*

95. Palisades, Idaho and Wyoming. *Oil and gas.*

96. Alton Hills, Utah. *Coal strip mine.*

97. Galveston Bay, Texas. *Supertanker port, coastal wetlands.*

98. Teton Wilderness, Wyoming. *Oil and gas.*

99. Matanuska Valley, Alaska. *Forest destruction, wood waste.*

100. Santa Maria Basin, California. *Offshore oil.*

101. Riverside County, California. *Development of raptor habitat.*

102. Deep Creek Roadless Area, Montana. *Oil and gas leasing.*

103. Kisaralik River, Alaska. *Hydroelectric project.*

104. Bob Marshall Wilderness, Montana. *Oil and gas leasing.*

105. Mendocino, California. *Historic building.*

106. South Carolina. *Billboards.*

107. Alaska railroad. *Herbicide spraying.*

108. Capitan Mountains, New Mexico. *Oil and gas leasing.*

109. Mountain lions, New Mexico. *Hunting in national park.*

110. Honey Springs, California. *Agricultural lands preservation.*

111. Oahe Reservoir, South Dakota. *Water for coal slurry line.*

112. Keynot Mine, California. *Cyanide leaching of gold.*

113. Little Granite Creek, Wyoming. *Oil and gas leasing.*

114. Truckee River, Nevada. *Endangered fish and irrigation.*

115. Channel Islands, California. *Oil and marine sanctuary.*

116. BLM lands, Nevada. *Grazing permits.*

117. Lake Meade, Arizona and California. *Mineral leasing in national recreation area.*

118. Susitna River, Alaska. *Hydroelectric project.*

119. Tulare Lake, California. *White bass, San Joaquin River.*

120. Panamint Dunes, California. *Off-road vehicles.*

121. Colorado wilderness. *Water rights for wilderness areas.*

122. Hallett Creek, California. *Water rights for wildlife.*

123. Perdido Key, Alabama. *Development in coastal floodplain.*

124. Matagorda Island, Texas. *Whooping cranes.*

125. Chula Vista, California. *Wetland protection.*

126. Lake Chelan National Recreation Area, Washington. *Land use, growth, logging.*

127. Algodunes Dunes, California. *Off-road vehicles.*

128. Gulf of Alaska. *Orca capture.*

129. Carquinez Strait, California. *Shell Oil, TOSCO water pollution.*

130. Western Hawaiian Islands. *Monk seals.*

131. Davis Canyon, Utah, and Hanford, Washington. *Nuclear waste.*

132. D'Arbonne National Wildlife Refuge, Louisiana. *Oil, gas, and woodpeckers.*

133. California desert. *Motorcycle race.*

134. Chugach National Forest, Alaska. *Forest planning.*

135. Santa Monica Bay, California. *Chevron water pollution.*

136. Santa Fe National Forest, New Mexico. *Archaeological sites.*

137. Fallon, Nevada. *Supersonic overflights by the Navy.*

138. Alaska national parks. *Mining access rights-of-way.*

139. Berner's Bay, Alaska. *Timber sale, logging roads.*

140. Upper Ouachita National Wildlife Refuge, Louisiana. *Oil, gas, and woodpeckers.*

141. Manistee and Huron National Forests, Michigan. *Land sale.*

142. National parks, Alaska. *Placer mining.*

143. Crawford, Nebraska. *Uranium mine, groundwater.*

144. San Pedro River, Arizona. *Minimum streamflow.*

145. Texas National Forests. *Pine beetle control.*

146. Adirondack State Park, New York. *Motors in wilderness.*

147. BLM lands, *Alaska. Placer mining.*

148. South Padre Island, Texas. *Transmission line.*

149. Grand Canyon, Arizona. *Tourist overflights.*

150. Mendocino County, California. *Motel/restaurant development.*

151. North St. Vrain Creek, Colorado. *Dam.*

152. Lake George, New York. *Herbicides for aquatic weeds.*

153. Sacramento, California. *Air pollution, agricultural land preservation.*

154. National forests, Colorado. *Fuelwood cutting.*

155. Presidio, San Francisco. *Post office construction.*

156. Sally Bell Grove, California. *Redwood logging.*

157. Shoshone National Forest, Wyoming. *Oil and gas leasing.*

158. Sitka, Alaska. *Pulp mill air pollution.*

159. Puget Sound, Washington. *Orca dart biopsies.*

160. Oahu, Hawaii. *Garbage incinerator.*

161. Chichagof Island, Alaska. *Hoonah-Tenakee logging road.*

162. Sweetwater Marsh, California. *Wetland preservation.*

163. Indiana. *State air pollution plan.*

164. Holy Cross Wilderness, Colorado. *Water rights.*

165. Sweeden's Swamp, Massachusetts. *Wetland preservation.*

166. Sabine River, Texas. *Wildlife refuge easement.*

167. Sierra Valley, California. *Offroad vehicle resort.*

168. Hart Mountain, Nevada. *Military overflights.*

169. Sacramento River, California. *Winter-run chinook salmon.*

170. National parks, Alaska. *Trespass cabins.*

171. Oakley, California. *Suburban sprawl.*

172. Arc Dome, Nevada. *Gold mine, access road.*

173. Virgin River, Utah. *Water rights.*

174. Domestic waters, offshore Alaska. *Driftnets & marine mammals.*

175. California desert. *Motorcycle race.*

176. North Bend, Oregon. *Water pollution.*

177. Sutherlin, Oregon. *Water pollution.*

178. Kissimee River, Florida. *River restoration.*

179. Rocky Flats, Colorado. *Nuclear waste burning.*

180. Baranof Warm Springs, Alaska. *Salmon farm.*

181. Sleeping Bear Dunes, Michigan. *Motorized vehicles.*

182. San Diego, California. *Air pollution—factory emissions.*

183. Burr Trail, Utah. *Road construction.*

184. California desert. *Motorcycle race.*

185. Port Townsend, Washington. *Water pollution.*

186. Longview, Washington. *Water pollution.*

187. Santa Barbara, California. *Offshore oil.*

188. Mt. Baker-Snoqualmie National Forest, Washington. *Olo Too timber sale.*

189. Siuslaw National Forest, Oregon. *Timber resales.*

190. San Francisco Bay, California. *Union Oil water pollution.*

191. Key West, Florida. *Wetland preservation.*

192. Cumberland Island National Seashore, Georgia. *Dredging.*

193. Everett, Washington. *Home port dredging.*

194. Idaho. *Water pollution standards.*

195. Colorado. *Water pollution standards.*

196. Hawaii. *Endangered plants.*

197. Maroon Bells, Colorado. *Mining road.*

198. Panhandle National Forest, Idaho. *Roadless areas.*

199. Tongass National Forest, Alaska. *Pulp company operating plan.*

200. Yukon-Kuskogwim, Alaska. *Mineral leasing.*

201. Owl Creek, California. *Old growth logging.*

202. Salmon Creek, California. *Old growth logging.*

203. Hampton Roads, Virginia. *Nuclear fuel shipment.*

204. Austin, Texas. *Airport.*

205. Everglades, Florida. *Water quality.*

206. Moreno Valley, California. *Growth control.*

207. Okanogan National Forest, Washington. *Logging.*

208. Holy Cross Wilderness, Colorado. *Water rights.*

209. Bureau of Land Management lands, Oregon. *Logging in spotted owl habitat.*

210. Northern California. *Roadside herbicide spraying.*

211. South Fork Trinity River, California. *Gulch, Flume-Wallow, Ridgeline, Dungeon, and Phantom timber sales.*

212. Mt. Hood National Forest, Oregon. *Fishhook Timber Sale.*

213. California national forests. *Acquisition of checkerboard inholdings.*

214. Olympic National Forest. *Soleduck timber sale.*

215. Anchorage, Alaska. *Highway easements.*

216. White Salmon, Washington. *Logging.*

217. Boca Raton, Florida. *Beach renourishment.*

218. Big Cypress National Preserve, Florida. *Oil and gas.*

219. Bridger-Teton National Forest, Wyoming. *Oil and gas.*

220. Caspar Creek, California. *Old growth logging.*

221. North Rim, Grand Canyon. *Hotel.*

222. Olympic National Forest, Washington. *Logging & spotted owls.*

223. Kachemak Bay, Alaska. *Shellfish farm.*

224. Mt. Hood National Forest, Oregon. *Badger Resell timber sale.*

225. Hilo, Hawaii. *Honolii power project.*

226. Elkhorn Ridge, California. *Old growth timber sale.*

227. San Francisco Bay Area, California. *Air pollution.*

228. Wrangell, Alaska. *Sawmill woodwaste.*

229. Maui, Hawaii. *Timber harvest.*

230. Colorado River. *Razorback sucker listing.*

231. Colorado River, Texas. *Concho water snake.*

232. Arctic National Wildlife Refuge. *Natural gas pipeline.*

233. Yellowstone National Park, Wyoming. *Log hauling.*

234. Penobscot River, Maine. *Basin Mills Dam.*

235. Bighorn National Forest, Wyoming. *Lodgepole pine regeneration.*

236. Northern Rockies. *Grizzly bear delisting.*

237. Horseshoe Meadow, California. *Recreational development.*

238. Sonoma County, California. *Vernal pools.*

239. Oregon Inlet, North Carolina. *Rock jetty.*

240. Rutland, Vermont. *Mall development in wetland.*

241. Shedd aquarium, Chicago. *False killer whale capture.*

242. Mount Graham, Arizona. *Endangered squirrel, observatory.*

243. Michigan. *Incinerator ash.*

244. Nevada County, California. *Steel-jawed traps.*

245. Rio Grande Valley, Texas. *Brush clearing.*

246. Merced River, California. *Hydroelectric project.*

247. Brookmont, Maryland. *Hydroelectric project.*

248. Ashley National Forest, Utah. *Forest plan appeal.*

249. Beaverhead National Forest, Montana. *Forest plan appeal.*

250. Bighorn National Forest, Wyoming. *Forest plan appeal.*

251. Chippewa National Forest, Minnesota. *Forest plan appeal.*

252. Croatan-Uwharrie National Forest, North Carolina. *Forest plan appeal.*

253. George Washington National Forest, Virginia. *Forest plan appeal.*

254. Gila National Forest, Arizona. *Forest plan appeal.*

255. Green Mountain National Forest, New Hampshire. *Forest plan appeal.*

256. Hoosier National Forest, Indiana. *Forest plan appeal.*

257. Humboldt National Forest, Nevada. *Forest plan appeal.*

258. Huron-Manistee National Forest, Michigan. *Forest plan appeal.*

259. Lincoln National Forest, New Mexico. *Forest plan appeal.*

260. Lewis and Clark National Forest, Montana. *Forest plan appeal.*

261. Mark Twain National Forest, Missouri. *Forest plan appeal.*

262. Medicine Bow National Forest, Wyoming. *Forest plan appeal.*

263. Monongahela National Forest, West Virginia. *Forest plan appeal.*

264. Ouachita National Forest, Arkansas. *Forest plan appeal.*

265. Ozark-St. Francis National Forest, Arkansas. *Forest plan appeal.*

266. Shawnee National Forest, Illinois. *Forest plan appeal.*

267. Shoshone National Forest, Wyoming. *Forest plan appeal.*

268. Sequoia National Forest, California. *Forest plan appeal.*

269. Superior National Forest, Minnesota. *Forest plan appeal.*

270. Toyiabe National Forest, Nevada. *Forest plan appeal.*

271. Apache-Sitgreaves National Forest, Arizona. *Forest plan appeal.*

272. Colville National Forest, Washington. *Forest plan appeal.*

273. Eldorado National Forest, California. *Forest plan appeal.*

274. Inyo National Forest, California. *Forest plan appeal.*

275. Los Padres National Forest, California. *Forest plan appeal.*

276. Plumas National Forest, California. *Forest plan appeal.*

277. San Bernardino National Forest, California. *Forest plan appeal.*

278. Wayne National Forest, Ohio. *Forest plan appeal.*

279. Arapaho and Roosevelt National Forests, Colorado. *Forest plan appeal.*

280. Clearwater National Forest, Idaho. *Forest plan appeal.*

281. Custer National Forest, Montana, North Dakota, South Dakota. *Forest plan appeal.*

282. Prescott National Forest, Arizona. *Forest plan appeal.*

283. Gulf Coast, offshore. *Oil and gas discharge permits.*

284. Big River, Rhode Island. *Dredge and fill permit.*

285. River of No Return. *Wilderness classification.*

286. Ohio River, Ohio and Kentucky. *Powerplants, air pollution.*

287. Beaver Creek Wilderness, Kentucky. *Strip mining.*

288. Bisti Badlands, New Mexico. *Mining in wilderness area.*

289. Moose Creek, Montana. *Timber sale in roadless area.*

290. Lassen National Forest, California. *Geothermal leasing adjacent to national park.*

291. Nevada BLM lands. *Wilderness inventory.*

292. Escudilla Mountain, Arizona. *Timber sale.*

293. West Chichagof/Yakobi Island, Alaska. *Management plan.*

294. Long Valley, California. *Geothermal leasing.*

295. Mount Palomar, California. *Logging.*

296. Salmon-Trinity Alps Primitive Area, California. *Trail protection.*

297. Mount Hood National Forest, Oregon. *Geothermal leasing.*

298. Blue Lake, Nevada. *Roadless area development.*

299. Walnut Creek, California. *Urban growth control.*

300. Westwood, California. *High-rise development.*

301. Middle Fork Eel River, Calfornia. *Logging along wild and scenic river.*

302. Rancho Seco Nuclear Power Plant, California. *Water pollution.*

303. Warm Springs Dam, California. *Salmon and steelhead habitat.*

304. Puget Sound, Washington. *Salmon farms.*

305. Riverside County, California. *Urban sprawl.*

306. Verdugo Hills, California. *Riparian habitat.*

307. Palm Springs, California. *Urban development.*

308. Gray Whale Ranch, California. *Timber sale.*

309. Oxnard, California. *Ocean pollution.*

310. Vallejo, California. *Agricultural land preservation.*

311. Tongass National Forest, Alaska. *Forest planning.*

312. Copper River, Alaska. *Wilderness preservation.*

313. Prince of Wales Island, Alaska. *Old growth logging.*

314. Little Book Cliffs, Colorado. *Oil and gas leasing.*

Oaks and sandstone wall, Lavender Canyon, Canyonlands National Park, Utah.

Sunrise on Hasselborg Lake, Admiralty Island, Alaska.

Wild by Law

was designed and produced by Herman + Company,
San Francisco, and printed in four-color process
lithography by Dai Nippon Printing Company, Tokyo.
The text was composed in Sabon by Mark Woodworth,
San Francisco. Maps created by Earth Surface Graphics.
The paper is OK Coat, 175 gsm.